PRINCE GEORGE'S COUNTY, MARYLAND

LAND RECORDS

1757-1759

Liber PP

Abstracted by

Michael R. Marshall

Colonial Roots
Millsboro, Delaware
2016

Colonial
Roots

Helping You Grow Your Family Tree

ISBN 978-1-68034-352-6

Printed November 2016

INTRODUCTION

This book has detailed abstracts of all 417 documents in Prince George's County, Maryland, Land Records Book PP - Maryland Archives microfilm CR 49525-2 (MSA CE65-17) recorded during the period of May 1757 through August 1759.

This volume contains details of land transactions, land divisions of estates, sales of lands seized for debts, marriage contracts, bills of sale, mortgages, entries of slaves, manumission of slaves, stray livestock, and depositions taken by the court.

The format of these abstracts generally follows the earlier Prince George's County land records that were published by T.L.C. Genealogy, Miami Beach, Florida, and who are no longer in business.

Notes with parenthesis "{ }" contain additional information or clarification.

Names are spelled as they appear. The most common usage was indexed.

Michael R. Marshall
October 2016

Page 1. At the request of Thomas Taylor the following Certificate of Stray was recorded May 20, 1757
PGCo Sct; I hereby certify that Thomas Taylor brought before me a stray bay mare between 12 and 13 hands high, not docked, nor branded, her right ear slight, a star in her forehead and a small white spot on her left nostril. Given under my hand this May 10, 1757, George Fraser

Page 1. At the request of Henry Lowe the following Deed was recorded May 21, 1757
Indenture made May 14, 1757 between John Abington, Gent and Mary Scott, Gentlewoman in consideration of 115 pounds sterling money of Great Britain paid by Henry Lowe, ordinary keeper, as also for divers other valuable considerations them hereunto moving, have sold a tract called "Carrick Fergus" containing 100 acres in fee simple and beginning at the second bound tree of Mr. Wade's land called "Friendship" and bounded by Mr. Hook's land called "Vainall," Kisconko Creek, "Locust Thickett" formerly the lands of Randolph Hinson. Signed John Abington, Mary Scott in the presence of and acknowledged before Peter Dent, George Fraser and at the same time Ann Abington, wife of John Abington, relinquished her right of dower.

Page 2. At the request of John Frazier the following Certificate of Stray was recorded May 23, 1757
PGCo Sct; I hereby certify that John Frazier living near the Eastern Branch ferry, brought before me a small sized black horse with a switch tail and branded on the near buttock and complains the said horse breaks into his inclosures. As witness my hand this May 19, 1756, David Ross

Page 2. At the request of Lawrence Spencer & Company the following Bill of Sale was recorded May 24, 1757

I, Hezekiah Magruder, planter in consideration of the sums of 6,121-1/2 pounds crop tobacco, 8 pounds 4 shillings and 4 pence current money, 30 pounds 4 shillings and 11 pence 3 farthings sterling paid by Lawrence Spencer & Company, merchants of Liverpool have sold Negroes Pris (21 yrs.) and Cate, 1 bay horse, 1 roan horse, 1 dark bay horse, 1 sorrel horse, 5 cows and calves, 3 heifers, 1 steer, 15 sheep, 8 chairs, 1 round table, 1 oval table, 3 pots, 1 frying pan, 1 large bed, 1 green rug, 2 blankets, 1 small bed, 2 blankets, 1 green rug, 2 bedstead and bed cords, 1-1/2 dozen pewter plates, 2 pewter dishes, 9 tin pans, 1 copper adz, 1 carpenter adz, 1 hand saw, 1 broad ax, 6 lopping axes, 6 hilling hoes, 4 weeding hoes, 2 flukes, 1 plow, 2 harrows, 1 pair iron tugs, 2 pair iron traces, 2 iron wedges, 1 gun, 16 cyder casks, 1 saddle and howsing, 1 small table, 1 small looking glass, 1 silk rug, 1 chest, 1 trunk, 1 corner cupboard, 1 tea kettle, 11 shoates, and 1 cart; provided nevertheless that Hezekiah Magruder will well and truly pay unto Lawrence Spencer & Company the above sums of tobacco and money on the June 1st next with legal interest, then this Bill of Sale shall cease. In witness whereof I have set my hand and seal this May 23, 1757, Hezekiah Magruder in the presence of and acknowledged before George Gantt

Page 3. At the request of Jeremiah Riley the following Deed of Gift was recorded May 25, 1757
I, Eliphaz Riley, for the love goodwill and affection which I do bear towards my well beloved son Jeremiah Riley and sundry other things me thereunto moving have given him part of a tract called "Hop Yard" containing 100 acres and lying on the north side of the Eastern Branch of Potomack River and bounded by Mr. William Young's corner tree called "The Neck" and the dividing line between Thomas Lucas and Eliphaz Riley. In witness whereof I have set my hand and seal this May 21, 1757, Eliphaz Riley, in the presence of and acknowledged before David Ross, Christopher Lowndes

Page 4. At the request of Edward Burch the following Certificate of Stray was recorded May 25, 1757

PGCo Sct; I hereby certify that Edward Burch brought before me a stray sorrel mare about 12-1/2 hands high, a blaze face, a small white spot on her off side and branded. Given under my hand this May 21, 1757, George Fraser

Page 4. At the request of James Marshall the following Bill of Sale was recorded May 30, 1757
I John Moore, Gentleman in consideration of 20 pounds current money of Maryland paid by James Marshall, merchant have sold Negro Michael (10 yrs.), 2 feather beds and furniture, 2 cows, 1 bay mare, provided nevertheless that if John Moore shall well and truly pay James Marshall the sum of 30 pounds current money upon May 1st next ensuing then this present Bill of Sale to be void. In witness whereof I have set my hand and seal this May 21, 1757, John Moore, in the presence of Thomas Smith Greenfield

Page 4. At the request of Thomas Talburt, Jr. the following Certificate of Stray was recorded June 2, 1757
PGCo Sct; Thomas Talburt, Jr. brought a stray sorrel mare about 13-1/2 hands high, star in her forehead, a small blaze in her face and branded on the near buttock. Given under my hand this May 30, 1757, George Fraser

Page 5. At the request of James Allin the following Certificate of Stray was recorded May 30, 1757
PGCo Sct; I hereby certify that James Allin brought before me a bay colt neither cut, docked or branded, about 2 or 3 years old and taken up as a stray. Joseph Belt, Jr.

Page 5. At the request of Theodore Venable the following Bill of Sale was recorded June 8, 1757
I John Brightwell in consideration of 800 pounds crop tobacco paid before December 25th next do sell unto Theodore Venable, planter, 2 heifers, 2 sows and pigs. In witness whereof I have set my hand and seal this May 30, 1757 John Brightwell in the presence of Thomas Brightwell, John Brightwell and acknowledged before George Gantt

3

Page 5. At the request of Reverend John Eversfield the following Deed was recorded June 8, 1757
Indenture made June 8, 1757, Edmund Casteel, planter in consideration of 520 pounds of transfer tobacco paid by Reverend John Eversfield, clerk have sold part of a tract called "Edmund's Frolick" containing 26 acres lying on the west side of Patuxent River and bounded by "Poormans Industry" lately conveyed by Casteel to said Eversfield. Signed Edmund Casteel in the presence of John Hepburn, John Stone Hawkins and acknowledged before John Hepburn and at the same time Rebecca Casteel wife of Edmund Casteel relinguished her right of dower

Page 6. At the request of Reverend John Eversfield the following Deed was recorded June 8, 1757
Indenture made June 8, 1757 between Edmund Casteel and Reverend John Eversfield, clerk, Whereas Edmund Casteel by deed of bargain bearing date January 31, 1756 did in consideration of 12 pounds sterling convey unto the said Eversfield in fee simple a tract called "Poormans Industry" containing 100 acres and part of another adjoining tract called "Casteel" containing 1 acre. But Edmund Casteel having proviso to the execution taken out at warrant of resurvey from the land office for the two tracts and united them under the name of "Edmund's Frolick" which differences of names my occasion disputes about the title of the land and for the remedying of such errors. Now this indenture witnesseth that Edmund Casteel in consideration of 12 pounds sterling money of Great Britain before these presents doth confirm and sell unto Reverend John Eversfield tracts called "Poormans Industry" and "Casteel" but now by resurvey called "Edmund's Frolick." Signed Edmund Casteel in the presence of John Hepburn, John Stone Hawkins and acknowledged before John Hepburn and at the same time Rebecca Casteel wife of Edmund Casteel relinguished her right of dower

Page 8. At the request of Hancock Lee the following Deed was

4

recorded June 9, 1757

Indenture made June 8, 1757, John Brightwell, Jr., planter in consideration of 30 pounds current money paid by Hancock Lee, merchant has sold part of a tract called "Cole Brooke" alias "Poplar Hills" now in the possession of Ann Brightwell containing 120 acres. Signed John Brightwell, Jr., in the presence of John Hepburn, William Turner Wootton and acknowledged before John Hepburn

Page 9. At the request of Joseph Sprigg the following Certificate of Stray was recorded June 11, 1757

I hereby certify that Joseph Sprigg brought before me a stray horse of a bright bay color, branded on the near buttock, about 14 hands high, one of his hind feet white, 8 or 9 years old and trimmed with the standing mane. June 9, 1757, J. Sprigg

Page 9. At the request of Henry Braddock the following Bill of Sale was recorded June 18, 1757

I Bartholomew Bolton, planter of PGCo in consideration of 20 pounds currency and 917 pounds of tobacco paid by Henry Braddock of Frederick County, Maryland, planter have sold 18 pewter plates, 3 pewter dishes, 2 basons, 1 pint mug, 1 tin coultinder, 1 tin pan, 1 quart tin sauce pan, 1 tin pot, 1 copper tea kettle, 1 tin funnel, 1 frying pan, 1 Dutch oven, 2 iron pots and hooks, 3 flesh forks, 1 iron ladle, 1 box iron and Healow, 1 looking glass, 1 spit, 2 beds with all the furniture, 1 corner cupboard, 13 Delph plates, ½ dozen tea cups and saucers, 2 teapots, 5 small bowls, 2 jugs, 1 mug, 12 small pigs, 1 man's saddle, 1 leather housing and bridle, 1 black horse colt, 3 forms, 2 buckets, two candle sticks, 2 tables, four chase, 5 stools, 1 pail, 4 tubs, 1 safe, 2 sifters, 1 broad tray, 2 pair traces, 2 blind bridles, 3 plows, 2 wedges, 2 hoes, 2 axes, 1 cyder cask, 1 pewter chamber pot, 1 adz. In witness whereof I have set my hand and seal this May 24, 1757, Bartholomew Bolton in the presence John England

Page 9. At the request of Josias Piles the following Bill of Sale was recorded June 20, 1757

I John Richardson, cooper, in consideration of 4 pounds current money of Maryland paid by Josias Piles, blacksmith, 4 sows, 3 white barrows and 12 shoates. In witness whereof I have set my hand and seal this June 14, 1757, John Richardson, in the presence of Timothy Drew

Page 9. At the request of Thomas Williams the following Certificate of Stray was recorded June 21, 1757
PGCo Sct; I hereby certify that Mr. Thomas Williams brought before me a small dark bay horse taken as a stray, branded on the off buttock, about 13 hands high, and has a saddle spot. June 16, 1757, Robert Tyler

Page 10. At the request of Edward Butt the following Deed was recorded June 25, 1757
I Thomas Butt, planter in consideration of the natural love and goodwill which I do bear unto my brother Edward Butt, planter and other good considerations me hereunto moving have given all that tract which my father Thomas Butt purchased of Samuel Swearingen containing 100 acres being the land whereon my father's late dwelling house now stands. In testimony whereof I have set my hand and seal this May 20, 1757, Thomas Butt, in the presence of and acknowledged before Mordecai Jacob, Thomas Williams

Page 10. At the request of Thomas Hamilton the following Certificate of Stray was recorded June 24, 1757
PGCo Sct, June 24, 1757; Thomas Hamilton brought before me as a stray a small black gelding about 12-1/2 hands high, branded on the near shoulder and thigh, and has saddle spots. Nathaniel Magruder

Page 10. At the request of Edward Mallow {Marlow?} the following Certificate of Stray was recorded June 28, 1757
Taken up by Edward Mallow, a small white mare, branded on the near buttock, paces slow, has a short switched tail. June 28, 1757, George Gantt

Page 11. At the request of George Naylor the following Deed was recorded June 28, 1757
Indenture made June 2, 1757, William Wheat, planter in consideration of 12 pounds current money paid by George Naylor, planter, has sold a tract called "Smith's Pasture" containing 50 acres and beginning at the southeast corner tree of "Stoke." Signed William Wheat, in the presence of John Hepburn, Richard Hoggins and acknowledged before John Hepburn

Page 12. At the request of Sarah Hughes the following Certificate of Stray was recorded June 28, 1757
PGCo Sct, June 24, 1757; Sarah Hughes brought a small bay mare before me as a stray branded on the near shoulder and near buttock and has a small star in her forehead. Thomas Williams

Page 12. At the request of Richard Hutton the following Land Commission was recorded abt June 28, 1757
Memorandum that on the special petition of Richard Hutton preferred to the justices of Prince George's County, Maryland on the 4th Tuesday in August in the 6th year of his Lordship commission the Right Hon. the Lord Proprietary Dominion etc., his Lordship commission issued by order of the justices aforesaid out of the county aforesaid on the 7th day of September Anno Domini 1757. In these words following, Frederick Absolute Lord and Proprietary of the Province of Maryland and Avalon Lord Baron of Baltimore vizt; to Messrs John Hawkins, Alexander Magruder, Thomas Letchworth and George Biggs of PGCo Gentleman, whereas Richard Hutton, is seized of a tract called "Ludford's Gift" and preferred his petition in writing to our county court held at Upper Marlborough Town before Peter Dent, Gentleman and his associates then and still justices within our county to examine evidence to prove and perpetuate the memory of the bounds of the said tract of land. Therefore, we command you any three or two of you to examine all witnesses or persons concerned touching their knowledge of the bounds of the said tract.

7

Witness John Contee, Gentleman, September 4, 1756. Issued September 7, 1756, Joseph Sim, Clk

Pursuant to a commission to examine evidences to prove the bounds of "Ludford's Gift" we hereby give notice that we intend to meet at the lands on Thursday, June 23rd next. Witness our hands and seals this May 14, 1757, Alexander Magruder, Thomas Letchworth, George Biggs

Maryland Sct; Frederick Absolute Lord and Proprietary of the Province of Maryland and Avalon Lord Baron of Baltimore vizt; to the sheriff of Anne Arundel County, Maryland greetings, we command you that you summon Martha George and William Read, Jr., that all excuses and delay be set aside they be and appear before the commissioners appointed to enquire concerning the bounds of "Ludford's Gift" on Thursday, June 23rd next. Issued June 20, 1757, Reverdy Ghiselin, Clk, Summoned John Raitt, Sheriff

PGCo Sct, June 23, 1757; Philip Willocy, aged 102 years or thereabouts being sworn deposeth that about 50 years ago as he was coming from Mr. Richard Clark's along the road he saw Samuel Waring, grandfather to the present Samuel Waring, who married a daughter of Arthur Ludford, and this deponent asked Waring what he was looking for who told him he was looking for his corner tree and clapped his arm around the white oak where he now stands, it standing on the north hill side of the road that leads from the main county road to the mouth of Fradsham alias Swanson's Creek and near a fork of the road which goes to Truman's Point and this deponent further saith not. Alexander Magruder, George Biggs

PGCo Sct, June 23, 1757; James Collings aged 34 years or thereabouts deposeth that as he and John George had been fishing and coming along the road, John George pointed at the tree where this deponent now stands and told him it was Samuel Waring's corner tree, it standing on the north hill side of the road that leads from the main county road to the mouth of Fradsham alias Swanson's Creek and near a fork of the road which goes to Truman's Point, it being a white oak. This deponent likewise says it was 20 years ago since he was shewed this tree and further saith not. Alexander Magruder, George

Biggs

PGCo Sct, June 23, 1757; William Read, Jr., of Anne Arundel County, Maryland, aged 26 years or thereabouts deposeth about 18 years ago he and his grandfather John George was going to a fishing when they came near the white oak where he now stands and slapped his left hand on it and said it was a bound tree of his land and at the same time extended his right hand which was towards the land called "Ludford's Gift" but at that time did not tell him what land it related to. The aforesaid tree stands on the north hill side of the road that leads from the main county road to the mouth of Fradsham alias Swanson's Creek and near a fork of the road which goes to Truman's Point and this deponent further saith not. Alexander Magruder, George Biggs

PGCo Sct, June 23, 1757; Paul Rawlings, Sr., aged 60 years or thereabouts deposeth that he was shown by his father this tree where he now stands and told by him that it was a bounded tree of Samuel Waring's land and old John Wilson and this deponent was out in the woods killing squirrels and said John Wilson shewed him the aforesaid tree and told him it was always deemed to be a corner tree of Samuel Waring's and it being a white oak and stands on a hill side and on the south side of a branch that falls into Fradsham alias Swanson's Creek below the land formerly belonging to Thomas Padgett and the said tree has a large bump growing out of the body on the north side and 5 feet from the root and he further declares it to be 46 years since he was shewed the aforesaid tree. Alexander Magruder, George Biggs

PGCo Sct, June 23, 1757; Paul Rawlings, Sr., aged 60 years or thereabouts deposeth that about 47 years ago, and as he, his father and John George were going fishing and coming near to the place where he now stands, they shewed him a bounded hickory and that it was the west corner tree of Mr. Craycroft's land and that Mr. Craycroft run from a pine by the marsh to the aforesaid tree (it being now down), it stood on the east side of the main county road that leads to Doves Bridges about 100 yards from the road and in the fork between the said road and the road that leads to Fradsham alias Swanson's Creek and within 20 yards of the northwest corner of an old field formerly known by the name of Hagathy's Old Field within 5 yards of a large stone at the root of a small white oak now marked as a memorandum and this deponent further saith not. Alexander Magruder, George Biggs

Page 14. At the request of Basil Waring the following Land Commission was recorded abt June 28, 1757

Memorandum that on the special petition of Basil Waring preferred to the justices of Prince George's County, Maryland on the 4th Tuesday in November in the 5th year of his Lordship commission the Right Hon. the Lord Proprietary Dominion etc., his Lordship commission issued by order of the justices aforesaid out of the county aforesaid on the 17th day of September Anno Domini 1755. In these words following, Frederick Absolute Lord and Proprietary of the Province of Maryland and Avalon Lord Baron of Baltimore vizt; to Messrs William Young, Walter Evans, John Wight and James White of PGCo Gentleman, whereas Henry Waring a minor under the care of Basil Waring, is entitled to part of a tract called "Jamaica Port Royal" and preferred his petition in writing to our county court held at Upper Marlborough Town for a commission to examine evidences to prove and perpetuate the memory of the bounds of the said tract of land. Therefore, we command you any three or two of you to examine all witnesses or persons concerned touching their knowledge of the bounds of the said tract. Witness John Contee, Gentleman, September 4, 1756. Issued September 7, 1756, Joseph Sim, Clk

By virtue of a commission to examine evidences to prove the bounds of "Jamaica Port Royal" we hereby give notice that we intend to meet at the lands on Monday, June 21st next at the dwelling plantation of William Pearce. Witness our hands and seals this May 15, 1757, William Young, James White

Then being at a bounded hickory the several witnesses were sworn;

June 21, 1756; Ninian Tannehill aged 64 years deposeth that by the deed of his land he was to run to a bounded hickory standing in the line of John Pierce's land and the said hickory was deemed to be a bounded tree and further saith not.

June 21, 1756; John Flint aged 66 years deposeth that by information of Charles Beall at the end of 320 perches from the end of the first line of "Widows Mile" he would find a bounded hickory which was the corner tree of Pierce and Hawkins land and further saith not. Then adjourned to the second Tuesday in August next

August 10, 1756; John Allison aged about 77 years saith that 30 odd years ago he took up 70 acres of land Capt. Archibald Edmonston being surveyor and running the first line came to the aforesaid hickory and Edmonston told him that it was the beginning tree of Pierce and Hawkins land, the deponent being at a bounded black oak about 50 yards from the main road that leads from George Town to Bladensburg and about 40 yards from the main branch of Goose Creek said that John Flint shewed him the aforesaid tree for a corner tree of the aforesaid land and further saith not.

August 10, 1756; William Barker aged about 38 years saith that about a year ago Thomas Lucas (since deceased) shewed him the black oak sapling as the beginning tree of Pierce and Hawkins land. Being at a bounded hickory he saith that said Lucas came here and said it was the fourth tree of the aforesaid land going from thence to a black oak described above. Going from thence to a small old field this deponent saith that within 15 yards of where he then stood Lucas shewed him the blaze where a bound tree of the aforesaid land formerly stood and did understand it to be the second tree of the said land and further saith now. Then adjoined to the first Tuesday in October, met and adjourned to November 15th.

November 15, 1756; James Burns aged 36 years declares about 8 months ago, Thomas Lucas, Sr., shewed him a bounded hickory which he said was the beginning tree of "Jamaica Port Royal"

November 15, 1756; Basil Waring aged about 43 years deposeth that about 12 months before he was at Mr. William Pierce's, a tenant of the said Waring's, that at the request of Mr. Thomas Lucas (since deceased) met him there and went to a small Spanish oak marked with the letter "L" and told him it was

11

the first bounded tree of "Jamaica Port Royal." The deponent being sworn at a piece of old field within about 30 yards of a large hickory being the beginning tree of William Harvie's land and says that about 12 months ago Thomas Lucas (since deceased) told him he saw the line run from the first Spanish oak and the course and number of perches ended in that pale being a small sunken in place to the south of the hickory. The deponent being sworn at a bounded black oak about 50 yards from the main road that leads from George Town to Bladensburg and about 40 yards from the main branch of Goose Creek said that about 12 months ago Thomas Lucas showed him that tree for the third bounded tree of "Jamaica Port Royal." The above deponent being sworn saith about 50 yards from a bound hickory about WNW where we laid a heap of stones that said Lucas told him he saw the standing. Afterwards it was cut down and made into fence logs and further saith not. Adjourned to the first Monday in December, met and adjourned to the third Tuesday in March

March 15, 1757; Leonard Brooke aged 29 years deposeth that about 18 months ago Thomas Lucas told him that the Spanish oak he was now at was the beginning tree of Mr. Hawkins and Pierces land and that he put a letter "L" on it. The deponent being sworn at a piece of old field within 30 yards of a large hickory being the beginning tree of William Hawkins land and says about 18 months ago Thomas Lucas said he saw Thomas Hodgkin's run the said line and ended there and said there stood the second tree of said land. The deponent being sworn at a bounded black oak about 50 yards from the main road that leads from George Town to Bladensburg and about 40 yards from the main branch of Goose Creek said that about 18 months ago Thomas Lucas showed him that tree for the third bounded tree of Hawkins and Pierce's land. The deponent being sworn saith that were put a heap of stones saith that Thomas Lucas came to that place and said that hereabouts stood the fourth tree of said land. William Young, Walter Evans, James White, John Wight

Page 16. At the request of Lawrence Spencer & Company the

following Bill of Sale was recorded June 30, 1757

I George Naylor, Jr., planter in consideration of the sums of 1118 pounds of crop tobacco and 4 pounds 13 shillings and 9 pence farthing current money paid by Lawrence Spencer & Company have sold Negro girl Lett now living at my father James Naylor's of Charles County, Maryland, provided nevertheless that if he shall well and truly pay unto Lawrence Spencer & Company the above sums of tobacco and money on July 10th next then the above Bill of Sale to be void. In witness whereof I have set my hand and seal this June 8, 1757, George Naylor, Jr., in the presence of John Hepburn, Samuel Hepburn and acknowledged before John Hepburn

Page 17. At the request of Stephen West the following Mortgage was recorded June 30, 1757

Indenture made June 29, 1757, Thomas Clagett, planter in consideration of 59 pounds 10 shillings and 10 pence current money paid by Stephen West, merchant has sold six Negroes; Nell (25 yrs.) and her children Ned (5 yrs.) and Sam (2 yrs.), also Jack (10 yrs.), Jim (12 yrs.) and Clare (11 yrs.), provided nevertheless that if Thomas Clagett shall well and truly pay unto Stephen West at or upon October 1st next the said sum of money with legal interest then this deed to be void. In witness whereof I have set my hand and seal this June 29, 1757, Thomas Clagett in the presence of Thomas Williams, David Craufurd and acknowledged before Thomas Williams

Page 18. At the request of Stephen West the following Bill of Sale was recorded June 30, 1757

I Henry Woolsford in consideration of 15 pounds current money paid by Stephen West of Upper Marlborough Town, merchant do sell 1 dark bay plough horse, 1 black mare, 1 horse colt, 1 young horse colt, 2 cows and 2 calves, 1 yearling steer, 1 yearling heifer, 1 feather bed, a suit of green curtains and furniture, 2 rugs and a pair of sheets, bedstead and all furniture belonging. In witness whereof I have set my hand and seal this June 19, 1757, Henry Wilsford, in the presence of Robert Tyler, Eleanor Tyler and acknowledged before Robert Tyler

Page 18.   At the request of William Dove the following Certificate of Stray was recorded June 30, 1757
I hereby certify that William Dove brought before me a stray black mare about 13 hands high, well set, branded on the near buttock. June 28, 1757, J. Sprigg

Page 18.   At the request of Zachariah Scott the following Certificate of Stray was recorded June 30, 1757
PGCo Sct; Zachariah Scott brought before me a black mare about 12 hands high branded on the off buttock, a switch tail and has a young colt. Also a black mare about 12 hands high branded on the near buttock with a switch tail and complains they are troublesome and breaks into his inclosures. Given under my hand this June 29, 1757, Christopher Lowndes

Page 19. At the request of James Ryan the following Certificate of Stray was recorded July 3, 1757
I hereby certify that James Ryan brought before me a stray small dark mare, branded on the near buttock and a small star in her forehead. Given from under my hand this July 1, 1757, J. Sprigg

Page 19. At the request of Henry Duly the following Deed was recorded July 8, 1757
Indenture made July 8, 1757, William Foard and Elizabeth Foard his wife, planter in consideration of 4000 pounds of tobacco paid by Henry Duly has sold part of a tract called "Turkey Thickett" containing 50 acres. Signed William Foard, in the presence of John Hepburn, James Young and acknowledged before John Hepburn and at the same time Elizabeth Foard wife of William Foard relinguished her right of dower

Page 20.   At the request of Benjamin Truman the following Supersedes was recorded July 11, 1757
You Benjamin Truman, John Johnson and William Bright do confess judgment to Peregrine Mackaness for the sum of 1 pound 14 shillings and 6 pence debt and 10 shillings and 6 pence costs currency which sums were recovered on July 12, 1757 before me one of His Lordships Justices of the Peace to be

levied on your goods chattels lands or tenements for the use of Peregrine Mackaness in case Benjamin Truman shall not pay and satisfy the said sum and costs thereon on February 10th next. Thomas Contee

Page 20. At the request of John Summers the following Certificate of Stray was recorded July 17, 1757
PGCo Sct; I hereby certify that John Summers, Sr., by his son Joseph Summers brought before me a small gray horse as a stray and made oath that it trespasses often on his father's plantation by getting into his cornfield. He is about 12 hands high, short docket, trimmed main and branded on the near shoulder. George Gordon

Page 20. At the request of William Steuart the following Supersedes was recorded August 6, 1757
You William Steuart, William Bright and George Naylor do confess judgment to John Frazier for the sum of 16 shillings currency which sum was recovered on July 12, 1757 before me one of His Lordships Justices of the Peace to be levied on your goods chattels lands or tenements for the use of John Frazier in case William Steuart shall not pay and satisfy the said sum and costs thereon on February 10th next. Thomas Contee

Page 20. At the request of Benjamin Early the following Certificate of Stray was recorded August 8, 1757
August 8, 1757, this day Benjamin Early brought before me a dark bay mare, 3 years old, branded on the near buttock, docked and has a star in her forehead and is troublesome to his plantation. Thomas Contee

Page 21. At the request of Thomas Davis the following Certificate of Stray was recorded August 13, 1757
August 20, 1757, Thomas Davis brought before me a dark bay mare, 3 years old, neither docket nor branded, has two white feet behind and a small blaze down her face, he complains she jumped in his cornfield. Thomas Contee

Page 21. At the request of John Waters, Jr. the following Deed was recorded August 13, 1757
Indenture made this July 20, 1757, Samuel Waters, Sr., planter in consideration of 4 pounds current money already paid by John Waters, Jr., planter, has sold part of a tract called "Cherry Walk" containing 37 acres and bounded by "Jericho." Signed Samuel Waters, in the presence of and acknowledged before Mordecai Jacob, Thomas Williams and at the same time Arteridge Waters wife of Samuel Waters relinguished her right of dower

Page 22. At the request of Christopher Edelen & Charles Edelen the following Deed of Division was recorded August 16, 1757
This indenture of division made between Christopher Edelen and Elizabeth Edelen his wife of one part and Charles Edelen and Catherine Edelen his wife of the other part. Witnesseth whereas Thomas Edelen, deceased father to said Christopher Edelen and Charles Edelen did by his last will and testament bequeath to them part of tracts called "Appledore" and "Rome" contiguous to each other and to be divided between them. Now know ye that Christopher Edelen and Elizabeth Edelen his wife and Charles Edelen and Catherine Edelen his wife by mutual consent and agreement have divided the two tracts in manner and form following; Charles Edelen and Catherine Edelen to have that part of "Appledore" now liveth and bounded by "Hawkins Lott" and Butler's Branch and the remaining part of "Appledore" lying on the northwest part together with "Rome to be the property of Christopher Edelen and Elizabeth Edelen. In witness whereof we have hereunto set our hands and affixed our seals this August 15, 1757, Christopher Edelen, Elizabeth Edelen, Charles Edelen, Catherine Edelen in the presence of John Frederick Augustus Priggs, Nicholas Dawson, James Edelen

Page 23. At the request of John Belt, Jr. the following Certificate of Stray was recorded August 16, 1757
PGCo Sct, August 19, 1757; I hereby certify that John Belt, Jr., brought a small sorrel horse before me as a trespasser and stray

16

branded on the near buttock and has a small star on her forehead. Thomas Williams

Page 23.   At the request of John Brashear son of John the following Bill of Sale was recorded August 20 1757
I John Brashear, Sr., in consideration of 38 pounds 13 shillings sterling paid by John Brashear son of John, has sold Negro Ned, 1 bed and furniture, 1 hand mill, 3 iron pots and pot rack, 1 cyder mill. In witness whereof I have set my hand and seal this August 13, 1757, John Brashear in the presence of and acknowledged before Mordecai Jacob, Thomas Mullikin

Page 23.   At the request of Francis Piles the following Supersedes was recorded August 23, 1757
You Francis Piles, Henry Darnall, Timothy Drue (Drew) do confess judgment to Joseph Adams for the sum of 1 pound 19 shillings and 7 pence currency which sums were recovered on August 18, 1757 before me one of His Lordships Justices of the Peace to be levied on your goods chattels lands or tenements for the use of Joseph Adams in case Francis Piles shall not pay and satisfy the said sum and costs thereon on February 10th next. George Gordon

Page 24. At the request of Joseph Wright the following Deed was recorded August 23, 1757
Indenture made August 23, 1757, Samuel Wright of Charles County, Maryland in consideration of 25 pounds sterling paid by Joseph Wright of Prince George's County, Maryland, planter, has sold part of "The Forrest" containing 100 acres and beginning at the beginning tree of "The Forrest" then running John Smith's given line and all the lands lying on the east side of Zachia Creek that I have in possession. Signed Samuel Wright in the presence of John Hepburn, William Thomas and acknowledged before John Hepburn

Page 24. At the request of Jasper Manduit the following Bill of Sale was recorded August 23, 1757
PGCo Sct; I Joseph Smith in consideration of 1773 pounds of

crop tobacco paid by Alexander Jackson have sold 1 dark gray mare, 1 small mare colt, 2 cows, a young heifer and 2 yearling, 7 head of sheep, 12 hogs and all my crop in ye house and household furniture and plantation utensils. In witness whereof I have set my hand and seal this May 3, 1757, Joseph Smith, in the presence of James Willson, Thomas Hilleary

On the back of which Bill of Sale was this indorsed, vizt. I do hereby assign all my right title and interest of the within Bill of Sale to Jasper Manduit, his heirs or assigns forever as witness my hand this 16th day of August 1757, Alexander Jackson, Test; Andrew Beall

Page 25. At the request of James Edelen the following Land Commission was recorded abt August 23, 1757

Memorandum that on the special petition of Richard Hutton preferred to the justices of Prince George's County, Maryland on the 4th Tuesday in November in the 6th year of his Lordship commission the Right Hon. the Lord Proprietary Dominion etc., his Lordship commission issued by order of the justices aforesaid out of the county aforesaid on the 16th day of December Anno Domini 1756. In these words following, Frederick Absolute Lord and Proprietary of the Province of Maryland and Avalon Lord Baron of Baltimore vizt; to Messrs George Fraser, John Baynes, Luke Marbury and John Tolson of PGCo Gentleman, whereas James Edelen, is seized of a tract called "Friendship" and preferred his petition in writing to our county court held at Upper Marlborough Town before Peter Dent, Gentleman and his associates then and still justices within our county to examine evidence to prove and perpetuate the memory of the bounds of the said tract of land. Therefore, we command you any three or two of you to examine all witnesses or persons concerned touching their knowledge of the bounds of the said tract. Witness John Contee, Gentleman, December 2, 1756. Issued December 16, 1756, Joseph Sim, Clk

Advertisement, by virtue of a commission to examine evidences to prove the bounds of "Friendship" we hereby give notice that we intend to meet at the lands on Monday, July 11th next. Witness our hands and seals this June 14, 1757, Luke Marbury,

John Tolson

Being now at a bounded locust post standing on the south side of a road called the Ridge Road

July 16, 1757; John Lanham aged 68 years or thereabouts says some years ago Nehemiah Wade had a commission to prove the bounds of a tract of land called "Friendship" and that Mr. William Penson, deceased proved the spot where now is a locust post which the deponent has his hand on to be the first boundary of the aforesaid land

July 16, 1757; Edward Stonestreet aged about 53 years says that between 30-40 years ago Richard Wade, deceased, told him that the spot where now stands a locust post was the first boundary of the aforesaid land. We went thence to a bounded gum standing on the north side of a gully that leads into Henson Branch

July 16, 1757; Edward Stonestreet, aged before, says 30 odd years ago, Francis Coffer told him that the gum was a boundary of Capt. Wade's land, likewise a boundary of Coffer's tract now in possession of Edward Clarkson.

July 16, 1757; Mr. Alexander Norton aged 43 years says some years ago Mr. Nehemiah Wade had a commission to prove the bounds of a tract called "Friendship" and Mr. William Penson, deceased, proved that the gum tree was a bound tree of Wade's land and further saith not. We went thence to a locust post standing on a point near where Thomas Lanham formerly lived

July 16, 1757; John Lanham aged as before says that 40 odd years ago Thomas Dickeson, deceased, shewed this deponent a bounded red oak where now stands a locust post and told him it was a boundary of Captain Wade's land, likewise this deponent says that William Hunter, deceased told him it was a boundary of Capt. Wade's land. We went from thence to a locust post standing on a hill side on the north of where Thomas Dickeson lived.

July 16, 1757; John Lanham aged above says some years ago Mr. Nehemiah Wade had a commission to prove the bounds of a tract called "Friendship" and at the same time Mr. William Penson, deceased, proved the locust post where he now has his hand on was a boundary of Capt. Wade's land, and then the tree

19

was down but that notches to be seen and that it was a red oak and further saith not. As witness our hands and seals this 20th day of August, Luke Marbury, John Tolson

Page 27. At the request of William Eversfield the following Land Commission was recorded abt August 23, 1757

Memorandum that on the special petition of William Eversfield preferred to the justices of Prince George's County, Maryland on the 4th Tuesday in November in the 6th year of his Lordship commission the Right Hon. the Lord Proprietary Dominion etc., his Lordship commission issued by order of the justices aforesaid out of the county aforesaid on the 16th day of December Anno Domini 1756. In these words following, Frederick Absolute Lord and Proprietary of the Province of Maryland and Avalon Lord Baron of Baltimore vizt; to Messrs Samuel Roundell, Joseph Sim, William Deakins and Leonard Piles of PGCo Gentleman, whereas William Eversfield, is seized of a tract called "Brookefield" and preferred his petition in writing to our county court held at Upper Marlborough Town before Peter Dent, Gentleman and his associates then and still justices within our county to examine evidence to prove and perpetuate the memory of the bounds of the said tract of land. Therefore, we command you any three or two of you to examine all witnesses or persons concerned touching their knowledge of the bounds of the said tract. Witness Joseph Belt, Jr., Gentleman, December 2, 1756. Issued December 16, 1756, Joseph Sim, Clk

Advertisement, by virtue of a commission to examine evidences to prove the bounds of "Brookefield" we hereby give notice that we intend to meet at the lands on Thursday, August 11th next. Witness our hands and seals this June 29, 1757, Samuel Roundell, William Deakins

August 11, 1757; Mr. George Naylor aged about 40 years and being sworn at a white oak tree standing on a small hill about 50 yards from an orchard that belonged to Mr. Thomas Hodgkin, deceased and where a stone is this day fixed and about 250 yards from said Hodgkin's dwelling house almost facing the front door, declares that about 4 years ago Mr. Thomas Hodgkin, deceased told him that the white oak tree was the

beginning tree of "Brookefield" formerly belonging to Richard Lee, Esqr., and a bounded tree of that part of "Brookefield" belonging to the said Hodgkin. George Naylor, Samuel Roundell, William Deakins, Leonard Piles
August 11, 1757; Mr. William Deakins aged about 38 years deposeth the same as above.

Page 28. At the request of William Newman Dorsett the following Deed was recorded August 25, 1757
Indenture made August 25, 1757, Thomas Dorsett, planter in consideration of 6 shillings currency as also the natural love and affection which he hath and doth bear unto his son William Newman Dorsett and for divers other good causes and considerations him thereunto moving doth given part of a tract of land called "Calvert's Manor" containing 202 acres and beginning at the edge of an old field called Locust Thickett Old Field and running thence east and south till it intersects the main branch that runneth into Half Pone Creek, then running up the branch till it intersects land sold by William Groome to William Beanes. Signed Thomas Dorsett in the presence of and acknowledged before Thomas Williams, Thomas Contee and at the same time Mary Dorsett wife of Thomas Dorsett relinquished her right of dower

Page 30. At the request of James Marshall the following Bill of Sale was recorded August 26, 1757
I John Rivers, dancing master in consideration of 33 pounds 19 shillings and 4 pence currency money of Maryland paid by James Marshall have sold, 26 sheep, 5 cows and 3 calves, 2 yearlings, 1 steer, 26 hogs, 1 man servant named Alexander Abram, 1 white woman servant named Rachel, 1 woman servant named Joice Tamerlane, 2 beds and furniture, 6 chairs, 2 small tables, 1 large table, 1 desk, 2 tea tables, 1 kitchen table, 3 iron pots, 1 large iron pot, 2 pair of pot hooks, 2 iron pot racks, 1 dozen pewter plates, 3 pewter dishes, 1 dozen table knives and forks, 1 warming pan, 1 brass mortar and pestle, 1 brass kettle, 1 tin funnel, 1 tin cullender, 2 ploughs, 3 hoes, 1 ax, 1 garden spade, 2 flesh forks, 1 iron ladle, 1 grid iron, 6 pails and

6 piggins, 3 washing tubs, 1 small alarm clock, 2 coffee pots, 2 tea kettles, 2 brass candlesticks and 1 iron candlestick, 3 tin milk pans, 2 tin kettles, 1 dozen earthen plates, 2 earthen dishes, 1 lawn search, 1 large earthen pot, 3 stone pickle pots, 1 brass cock, 1 large china bowl, 1 china tea pot, 6 china coffee cups, 1 wooden trough containing 30 gallons of soft sope, 1 fire shovel and tongs, 18 petty pans, 2 flock beds and furniture, 2 smoothing irons and standard, 2 hammers, 1 mahogany waiter, 30 glass bottles, 2 bottles of laurel oil, 2 pewter basons, 3 oznaburg bags, 3 padlocks, 1 cow hide and the Indian corn and fodder growing in a field rented of Mr. Henry Rozer. In witness whereof I have set my hand and seal this August 24, 1757, John Rivers, in the presence of and acknowledged before Peter Dent

Page 31.   At the request of Thomas Smith Greenfield the following Supersedes was recorded August 26, 1757
You Thomas Smith Greenfield, William Bowie and Francis King do confess judgment to William Mackey for the sum of 31 pound 6 shillings and 2 pence and 280-3/4 pound tobacco and 6 pence currency which sums were recovered on the 4th Tuesday in August past to be levied on your goods chattels lands or tenements for the use of William Mackey in case Thomas Smith Greenfield shall not pay and satisfy the said sum and costs thereon on February 10th next. Thomas Contee

Page 31.   At the request of Eliphaz Riley the following Supersedes was recorded September 5, 1757
PGCo, September 3, 1757, Then Eliphaz Riley, Jeremiah Riley and Walter Evans superseded a judgment obtained by Richard Snowden against Eliphaz Riley at August Court last for 29 pound sterling and 260-3/4 pounds tobacco and all cost that shall hereafter arise. Christopher Lowndes, David Ross

Page 31.   At the request of Thomas Beane the following Certificate of Stray was recorded September 5, 1757
PGCo Sct, September 5, 1757; Thomas Beans brought before me an iron grey horse about 14 hands high, branded on ye off buttock and shoulder, he complains he is troublesome and

breaks into his inclosures. Christopher Lowndes

Page 31. At the request of Henry Threlkeld the following Deed was recorded September 5, 1757
Indenture made January 28, 1757, James Hopkins of the Parish of St. Martin in the Fields in the County of Middlesex, Surgeon, in consideration of 12 pounds lawful money of Great Britain paid by Henry Threlkeld, merchant, have sold a lot of land being near Bladensburg in PGCo containing 2 acres together with the tobacco warehouse erected on part of the premises which land and warehouse was late part of the estate of Mathew Hopkins, merchant, deceased brother of the said James Hopkins and now his heir at law. Signed James Hopkins in the presence of Jasper Manduit, George Crawford
I James Hopkins do appoint John Johnstown of the Parish of St. George Wapping my true and lawful attorney to acknowledge this deed
PGCo, July 22, 1757, Then Mr. Jasper Manduit came before us two of His Lordships Justices of the Peace and made oath that he saw James Hopkins execute the Power of Attorney and at the same time he saw George Crawford subscribe his name as witness. John Cooke, Christopher Lowndes
PGCo, July 22, 1757, Then Capt. John Johnstown came before us came before us two of His Lordships Justices of the Peace in behalf of James Hopkins acknowledged the within deed. John Cooke, Christopher Lowndes

Page 33. At the request of Nathaniel Offutt the following Deed was recorded September 7, 1757
Indenture made May 13, 1757; Joseph Belt, Gentleman and Margery Belt his wife of one part and Burgess Mitchell of the other part. Whereas Susanna Mitchell, widow, was seized of and estate of inheritance in fee tail in a tract called "Greenwood" the immediate reversion or remainder belongs to Burgess Mitchell, eldest son of said Susanna Mitchell, and whereas Susanna Mitchell by virtue of an act of assembly made at Annapolis the 6th day of October, 1724 entitled and Act for the Relief of Long Languishing Prisoners did convey unto Philip Lee, Gentleman

23

then sheriff of PGCo for and during the natural life of the said Susanna and whereas Philip Lee by his deed bearing date March 2, 1725 for the consideration of 51 pounds current money did convey the said tract of "Greenwood" unto Margery Sprigg, now wife of Joseph Belt for the natural life of Susanna Mitchell and whereas likewise Burgess Mitchell stands justly indebted to several of the inhabitants of this province in divers sums of money and tobacco which Burgess Mitchell and John Mitchell his son are willing and desirous should be bonafide paid and satisfied without docking the entail of the land so as to enable them to sell and convey the same and inheritance thereof to raise money for the end and purposes aforesaid. Now this indenture witnesseth that Joseph Belt and Margery Belt his wife for the consideration of the premise and the sum of 5 shillings current money have surrendered by these presents unto Burgess Mitchell upon the conditions hereinafter mentioned all that tract called "Greenwood" containing 380 acres to have and to hold during the natural life of Susanna Mitchell upon condition that Burgess Mitchell shall be made perfect tenant of the freehold and appear gratis to a writ or writs of entry and to vouch to warranty of John Mitchell son and heir apparent. Signed Joseph Belt, Margery Belt, in the presence of and acknowledged before John Sprigg, Joseph Belt, Jr., and at the same time Margery Belt wife of Joseph Belt relinquished her right of dower

May 13, 1757, received of Burgess Mitchell 5 shilling consideration money and received of Nathaniel Offutt 15 shilling and 2 pence half penny sterling for an alienation fine on the 380 acres.

Page 35. At the request of Thomas Vermillion the following Certificate of Stray was recorded September 20, 1757
PGCo Sct; I hereby certify that Thomas Vermillion brought before me a small bay mare about 11 hands, neither docked or branded and about 5 years old. September 17, 1757, J. Sprigg

Page 35. At the request of Benjamin Brookes the following Deed was recorded September 26, 1757

Indenture made July 11, 1757; Edward Clagett, planter in consideration of 32 pounds 10 shillings sterling money of Great Britain paid by Benjamin Brookes, planter and for divers other good causes and considerations him hereunto moving has sold a tract called "Fowlers Delight" containing 100 acres and formerly lying in Calvert County, Maryland but now in PGCo on the freshes of Patuxent River in the woods and on the west side of the Western Branch of said river. Beginning at the north west corner tree of Major Charles Boteler's land and binding on "Beall's Chance" Signed Edward Clagett, in the presence of George Clarke, John Hepburn and acknowledged before John Hepburn

Page 36. At the request of Abraham Barnes the following Mortgage was recorded September 26, 1757
Indenture made September 24, 1757; Thomas Standage of PGCo, in consideration of 3000 pounds of crop inspected tobacco in three hogshead 306 pounds of transfer tobacco, 6 pounds 9 shillings and 5 pence paper currency and 31 pounds 19 shillings and 9 pence sterling paid by Abraham Barnes of St. Mary's County, Maryland has sold part of a tract called "Discovery" made over and conveyed by William Masters to Ezekiel Goslin and by him made over to Thomas Standage and whereon he now dwells containing 126 acres. Also Negroes, Nan, Barbara, Grace and Jamey, 3 cows and calves, 2 steers, 1 heifer, 7 sheep, 3 lambs, 1 ram, 1 mare, 1 horse, together with all the dwelling houses, outhouses, fences, orchards belonging, provided that Thomas Standage shall well and truly pay unto Abraham Barnes the aforesaid sums of tobacco and money at or upon June 1, 1760 with legal interest then this indenture to be void.   Signed Thomas Standage, in the presence of and acknowledged before John Hepburn, William Thomas and at the same time Margaret Standage wife of Thomas Standage relinquished her right of dower

Page 37. At the request of Thomas H. Marshall the following Certificate of Stray was recorded October 7, 1757
PGCo Sct; Whereas Capt. Thomas H. Marshall brought before me

a middle sized well-made bay horse, a switch tail, hanging main and star in his forehead, about 7-8 years old, branded on the near buttock, troublesome by breaking into his pasture, has slow pace and gallops well. This is to certify that he has the liberty to confine and use the said horse until the owner can be found. Given under my hand this October 3, 1757, Peter Dent

Page 37. At the request of William Cross the following Certificate of Stray was recorded August 30, 1757
PGCo Sct, August 27, 1757; William Cross brought before me as a trespassing stray a middle sized bay horse, a blaze in his face, his hind feed white, no perceivable brand. Mordecai Jacob

Page 38. At the request of Benoni Price the following Certificate of Stray was recorded August 30, 1757
Benoni Price brought before me as a stray a small bay gelding about 12 hands high, has a blaze face, lately cut and docked, not branded, given under my hand this August 29, 1757, Nathaniel Magruder

Page 38. At the request of Joseph Walker the following Certificate of Stray was recorded October 11, 1757
PGCo Sct, October 8, 1757; Joseph Walker brought before me a small bay horse, branded on the near buttock, appears to be about 4 years old, likewise a sorrel colt, neither branded or docked, appears to be 2 years old as trespassers and strays. Mordecai Jacob

Page 38. At the request of Alexander Jackson the following Deed was recorded October 11, 1757
Indenture made August 13, 1757; Elisha Hoskinson of Frederick County, Maryland in consideration of 11 pound current money of Maryland and 1 barrel of corn paid by Alexander Jackson has sold a tract called "Beall's Mistake" containing 40 acres and bounded by "Elizabeth's Delight." Signed Elisha Hoskinson in the presence of and acknowledged before John Cooke, Christopher Lowndes and at the same time Ann Hoskinson wife of Elisha Hoskinson relinguished her right of dower

Page 39. At the request of John Clagett the following Supersedes was recorded October 13, 1757

You John Clagett, William Beanes, Jr., and Benjamin Berry, Jr., do confess judgment to James Russell for the sums of 43 pounds 10 shillings and 8 pence sterling and 12 pounds 12 shillings and 8 pence and 535-3/4 pounds of tobacco which sums were recovered on the 4th Tuesday in June last to be levied on your goods chattels lands or tenements for the use of James Russell in case John Clagett shall not pay and satisfy the said sum and costs thereon on February 10th next. Taken before us this October 13, 1757, Thomas Williams, John Contee

Page 39. At the request of Reverend John Eversfield the following Deed was recorded October 15, 1757

Indenture made October 13, 1757; William Miles in consideration of 10,600 pounds of transfer tobacco and 8 pound currency of Maryland paid by Reverend John Eversfield has sold two parts of two tracts, one called "Gedling" the other "Gedling and Archers Pasture" contiguous and adjoining each other, being the plantation whereon I now dwell on the west side of Patuxent River. "Gedling" containing 100 acres and bounded by "Quick Sale," Alexander Magruder's land called "Anchovies Hills." "Gedling and Archers Pasture" containing 77 acres and beginning at Alexander Magruder's land called "Anchovies Hills." Signed William Miles in the presence of and acknowledged before George Gantt, Thomas Contee and at the same time Margaret Miles wife of William Miles relinquished her right of dower

Page 40. At the request of William Jenkins the following Certificate of Stray was recorded October 20, 1757

October 14, 1757; William Jenkins brought before me as a stray an iron gray horse about 13 hands high, branded on the off thigh. Nathaniel Magruder

Page 41. At the request of Richard Hutton the following Deed was recorded October 20, 1757

Indenture made September 17, 1757; Stephen Yoe of Queen

Anne County, Maryland, planter in consideration of 20 pound current money paid by Richard Hutton, tailor, has sold all that moiety of a tract called "Ludford's Hope" containing 100 acres and lying on the west side of Patuxent River lying near "Ludford's Gift" and the lands formerly belonging to Michael Farmer, which moiety of "Ludford's Hope" formerly belonged to his grandfather Stephen Yoe and taken up by him in partnership with Arthur Ludford. Signed Stephen Yoe, in the presence of and acknowledged before Jonathan Nicols, William Banckes, JP's of Queen Anne County, Maryland

Page 42. At the request of Joseph Belt, Jr. the following Deed was recorded October 22, 1757
Indenture made September 26, 1757; Reverend John Orme, clerk, in consideration of 5 pound sterling money paid by Joseph Belt, Jr., miller, has sold part of a tract called "Collington" containing 3 acres and lying on the west side of the mill pond and binding on the line of 10 acres formerly sold out of the same tract for the use of a water mill thereon, and the line of 1 acre of land part of the same tract sold to Joseph Belt, Jr. as by deed from John Orme bearing date the 25th day of October, 1751. Together with all improvements belonging, reserving only a convenient road through the 3 acres between the dwelling house of Joseph Belt, Jr., and the bottom of the hill to the westward thereof. Signed John Orme, in the presence of John Hepburn, James Orme and acknowledged before John Hepburn and at the same time Ruth Orme wife of John Orme relinguished her right of dower

Page 43. At the request of Joseph Thompson the following Certificate of Stray was recorded October 22, 1757
PGCo Sct, October 19, 1759; taken up as a stray and brought before me a small bay mare not branded , with a short dock and some saddle spots on her back. George Gantt

Page 43. At the request of Benjamin Adams the following Certificate of Stray was recorded October 24, 1757
PGCo Sct, October 21, 1759; This is to certify that Benjamin

Adams brought before me as a stray a black mare colt that has trespassed upon him for two years past, branded on the near shoulder and buttock, about 12-1/2 hands high and no white about her. George Gordon

Page 43. At the request of Benjamin Adams the following Certificate of Stray was recorded October 27, 1757
PGCo Sct, October 26, 1759; Benjamin Adams brought before me as a stray and iron grey gelding about 12 hands high, branded on the near thigh. Nathaniel Magruder

Page 43. At the request of Morris Miles, Jr. the following Deed of Gift was recorded October 28, 1757
I Morris Miles, planter in consideration of the natural love and affection which I have and do bear unto my son Morris Miles, Jr., planter, and for and in consideration of 5 shillings current money have given all that tract called "Wickham's Purchase" containing 150 acres. Also Negroes, Sarah, Dinah, Sue, Fillis, Sarah, Lucy and Harry. Also all my stock of horses, cattle, sheep and hogs, household and kitchen furniture, provided that I Morris Miles shall peacefully and quietly enjoy the land, Negroes and furniture during my natural life. In witness whereof I have set my hand and seal this October 5, 1757, Morris Miles in the presence of John Hepburn, Leonard Oliver and acknowledged before John Hepburn

Page 44. At the request of William Turnor Wootton the following Deed of Gift was recorded October 31, 1757
Indenture made October 8, 1757; Between Turnor Wootton and Elizabeth Wootton his wife of one part and William Turnor Wootton of the other part. Witnesseth whereas Josias Willson, deceased, did by his last will and testament bequeath unto his wife, then Elizabeth Willson now the wife of Turnor Wootton the one moiety of his land called "Land Over." Now this indenture witnesseth that Turnor Wootton and Elizabeth Wootton his wife in consideration of 5 shillings and the love and good will that they have unto William Turnor Wootton and divers other considerations doth give the aforesaid moiety of

29

land called "Land Over" containing 320-1/2 acres. Signed Turnor Wootton, Elizabeth Wootton in the presence of and acknowledged before Thomas Williams, Robert Tyler and at the same time Elizabeth Wootton wife of Turnor Wootton relinguished her right of dower

Page 45. At the request of Lancelot Wilson the following Deed was recorded November 1, 1757
Indenture made August 27, 1757; Joseph Wilson in consideration of 10 pound sterling paid by Lancelot Wilson, planter, has sold parts of two tracts, one called "Thomas & Mary" and the other "Wilson's Enlargement" containing 31 acres. Signed Joseph Wilson, in the presence of and acknowledged before John Cooke, Thomas Williams and at the same time Mary Wilson wife of Joseph Wilson relinguished her right of dower

Page 45. At the request of Joseph Wilson the following Deed was recorded November 1, 1757
Indenture made August 27, 1757; Lancelot Wilson, planter in consideration of 10 pound sterling paid by Joseph Wilson, planter, has sold part of "Wilson's Enlargement" beginning at the 5th line of "Thomas & Mary" and containing 28 acres. Signed Lancelot Wilson in the presence of and acknowledged before John Cooke, Thomas Williams and at the same time Elizabeth Wilson wife of Lancelot Wilson relinguished her right of dower

Page 47. At the request of Benjamin Beckett the following Certificate of Stray was recorded November 2, 1757
PGCo Sct, October 31, 1759; Benjamin Beckett brought before me as a trespasser and stray a small bay mare, 3 years old, docked by no visible brand. Mordecai Jacob

Page 47. At the request of Nathaniel Offutt the following Deed was recorded November 5, 1757
Indenture made October 31, 1757; Joseph Belt, Gentleman and Margery Belt his wife in consideration of 50 pounds sterling paid by Nathaniel Offutt as also for divers other good causes and

considerations them thereunto moving have sold part of a tract called "Greenwood" containing 100 acres during the natural life of Susanna Mitchell. Signed Joseph Belt, Margery Belt in the presence of and acknowledged before Joseph Belt, Jr., J. Sprigg and at the same time Margery Belt wife of Joseph Belt relinguished her right of dower

Page 49. At the request of Nathaniel Offutt the following Deed was recorded November 5, 1757
This Indenture Tripartite made Mary 14, 1757; between Burgess Mitchell, planter of the first part, John Mitchell, planter and son and heir of Burgess Mitchell of the second part and Nathaniel Offutt, Gentleman of the third part. Whereas Joseph Belt and Margery Belt his wife by deed of surrender bearing date May 13, 1757 between them and Burgess Mitchell reciting that whereas Susanna Mitchell, widow, was seized of an estate of inheritance in a tract called "Greenwood" and the immediate reversion or remainder belongs to Burgess Mitchell's eldest son, and whereas Susanna Mitchell by virtue of an act of assembly made at Annapolis the 6th day of October, 1724 entitled and Act for the Relief of Long Languishing Prisoners did convey unto Philip Lee, Gentleman then sheriff of PGCo for and during the natural life of the said Susanna and whereas Philip Lee by his deed bearing date March 2, 1725 for the consideration of 51 pounds current money did convey the said tract of "Greenwood" unto Margery Sprigg, now wife of Joseph Belt for the natural life of Susanna Mitchell and whereas likewise Burgess Mitchell stands justly indebted to several of the inhabitants of this province in divers sums of money and tobacco which Burgess Mitchell and John Mitchell his son are willing and desirous should be bonafide paid and satisfied without docking the entail of the land so as to enable them to sell and convey the same and inheritance thereof to raise money for the end and purposes aforesaid. in consideration of the premises and the sum of 5 shillings current money and for perfecting some conveyance shortly to be made by Burgess Mitchell by way of common recover and proper deed have surrendered by these presents unto Burgess Mitchell upon the

31

conditions hereinafter mentioned all that tract called "Greenwood" containing 380 acres to have and to hold during the natural life of Susanna Mitchell upon condition that Burgess Mitchell shall be made perfect tenant of the freehold and appear gratis to a writ or writs of entry and to vouch to warranty of John Mitchell son and heir apparent to enable him to sell and dispose of the inheritance. Now this indenture witnesseth that Burgess Mitchell in consideration of 70 pounds sterling and 5000 pounds of tobacco paid by Nathaniel Offut as also in consideration of 2000 pounds tobacco paid to John Mitchell by Nathaniel Offutt, they the said Burgess Mitchell and John Mitchell shall and will before the end of next Provincial Court permit and suffer the said Nathaniel Offutt to sue and prosecute one or more writ or writs of Entry Sur Desseisin in the post returnable before the Justices of the Provincial Court of Maryland against them of all and singular the lands and premises above mentioned. Signed Burgess Mitchell, John Mitchell in the presence of and acknowledged before Joseph Belt, Jr., J. Sprigg and at the same time Catharine Mitchell wife of Burgess Mitchell and Mary Mitchell wife of John Mitchell relinguished their right of dower

Page 51. At the request of Richard Simmons the following Deed was recorded November 12, 1757
Indenture made October 28, 1757; James Wilson, planter and Mary Wilson his wife in consideration of 150 pounds sterling of Great Britain paid by Richard Simmons, planter, has sold part of a tract called "Land Over" containing 320-1/2 acres and beginning at the south west corner of Thomas Hilleary's land called "Three Sisters." Signed James Wilson, in the presence of and acknowledged before Mordecai Jacob, Thomas Williams and at the same time Mary Wilson wife of James Wilson relinguished her right of dower

Page 53. At the request of Leonard Oliver the following Deed was recorded November 14, 1757
Indenture made October 25, 1757; John Hunt of Charles County, Maryland, planter, in consideration of 1800 pounds transfer

crop tobacco paid by Leonard Oliver, planter of PGCo, has sold a tract called "Kent's Chance" containing 100 acres and lying in Charles County, Maryland and PGCo on the west side of the Patuxent River in the woods in the freshes near that branch of Swanson's Creek called Boulton's Branch and to the westward of the Hugh Stone's land called "Diggbeth." (Originally granted unto Robert Kent and by his verbal will to Joseph Fry and by him to his son Robert Fry and by him to his son Joseph Fry and by him conveyed to John Hunt the grantor to his deed). Signed John Hunt in the presence of John Hepburn, Joseph Yates and acknowledged before John Hepburn and at the same time Esther Hunt wife of John Hunt relinguished her right of dower

Page 54. At the request of Benedict Calvert, Esqr., the following Land Commission was recorded abt November 14, 1757
Memorandum that on the special petition of Benedict Calvert, Esqr. preferred to the justices of Prince George's County, Maryland on the 4th Tuesday in June in the 7th year of his Lordship commission the Right Hon. the Lord Proprietary Dominion etc., his Lordship commission issued by order of the justices aforesaid out of the county aforesaid on the 30th day of June Anno Domini 1757. In these words following, Frederick Absolute Lord and Proprietary of the Province of Maryland and Avalon Lord Baron of Baltimore vizt; to Messrs John Hepburn, Robert Bradley, Francis King, Joseph Sim of PGCo Gentleman, whereas Benedict Calvert, Esqr., is seized of a tract called "Lodge" and preferred his petition in writing to our county court held at Upper Marlborough Town before Peter Dent, Gentleman and his associates then and still justices within our county to examine evidence to prove and perpetuate the memory of the bounds of the said tract of land. Therefore, we command you any three or two of you to examine all witnesses or persons concerned touching their knowledge of the bounds of the said tract. Witness John Contee, Gentleman, June 30, 1757. Issued July 7, 1757, Joseph Sim, Clk
By virtue of a commission to examine evidences to prove the bounds of "Lodge" we hereby give notice that we intend to meet at the lands on August 16th. Witness our hands and seals this

33

July 23, 1757, John Hepburn, Joseph Sim

Robert Mills aged about 60 years first sworn at a black oak standing on the west side of a hill and the east side of a branch that runs into Charles Branch declares that about 30 years ago on the first day of April, Capt. Walter Hoxton sent for him and carried him to this black oak standing between the plantation formerly in the possession of John Miller and the land belonging to Moses Orme and this deponent carried the chain on a survey made for Mr. John Hyde on land sold him by Henry Darnall, Esqr., deceased, and when then came to this black oak Walter Hoxton caused 12 notches to be made on the tree. They then left supposing they had their quantity of land but this deponent understood when they came to plat the land they had run, there was 500 acres wanting of the complement and afterwards in order to add the 500 acres they began at a beech standing near the plantation of Mr. Charles Beaven and near Charles Branch and then they laid off the aforesaid 500 acres and this deponent further saith not. Given under our hands and seals this August 16, 1757, Robert Mills, John Hepburn, Robert Bradley, Joseph Sim

Charles Beaven aged about 60 years declares the aforesaid black oak standing near Charles Branch bounded in presence of Walter Hoxton and several others was a boundary of the land sold John Hyde by Henry Darnall, Esqr., deceased, but did not know what tree it was of the said land and this deponent saith that some time afterwards hen Mr. Henry Massey acted as attorney in fact for Samuel Hyde son of John Hyde, deceased, the aforesaid Massey came to this deponent and desired him to shew him the aforesaid bounded black oak which he did. They then began and the tree to run out but after they had run some distance he told Mr. Massey he was certainly wrong as he ran into lands sold some time before by Col. Henry Darnall, deceased. Massey then looked at the courses and said they were the courses he must run and went on until they came to the main road near Mr. James Brooke's. It being near night they left off and further saith not. Given under our hands and seals this August 16, 1757, Charles Beaven, John Hepburn, Robert Bradley, Joseph Sim

Thomas Taylor, tanner, aged about 50 years, being at the aforesaid black oak, declares he was employed by Mr. Massey to carry the chains in running out Mr. Hyde's land and they began at the black oak standing near Charles Branch and run until they came to Piscattaway Branch and left off. This deponent further saith he was on the said land when Mr. Calvert begun from said tree and that he run until they came into Mr. Ignatius Digges plantation and this deponent then understood they were running into elder surveys and they then left off, and further this deponent saith not. Given under our hands and seals this August 16, 1757, Thomas Taylor, John Hepburn, Robert Bradley, Joseph Sim

Samuel Lusby aged about 26 years, being at the aforesaid black oak, declares he was present when Mr. Hodgkin, deceased, begun at the black oak near Charles Branch in order to make a survey and that Mr. Stephen West was present and his people carried the chain. He was told by Mr. Hodgkin that the black oak was called the beginning tree of Hyde's land and that Mr. West was not in hearing at the time he asked Mr. Hodgkin whether they begun at the black oak and further saith not. Given under our hands and seals this August 16, 1757, Samuel Lusby, John Hepburn, Robert Bradley, Joseph Sim

Henry Darnall, Esqr., aged about 53 years, being at the aforesaid black oak, declares that he attended on the survey of a parcel of land sold by Henry Darnall, Esqr., deceased, (his father) to John Hyde that he remembers they began somewhere on Charles Branch to lay out the land but does not know what place but he remembers that the parties agreed in laying off the quantity of land sold as aforesaid to run clear of Arnold Livers and John Miller's land sold them by Col. Henry Darnall, deceased and Henry Darnall, Esqr., deceased and further saith not. Given under our hands and seals this August 16, 1757, Henry Darnall, John Hepburn, Robert Bradley, Joseph Sim, and we then adjourned until August 22 [sic 20], 1757

Moses Orme, aged about 64 years being sworn at a dead lying white oak very near a small branch with three notches, declares that about 20 years ago John Miller, deceased, told him that the marked white oak was a bounded tree of his land and further

35

saith not. Given under our hands and seals this August 20, 1757, Moses Orme, Robert Bradley, Joseph Sim

Charles Beaven aged about 60 years being at the aforesaid white oak, declares that John Miller, deceased, had often times told him that Mr. Henry Darnall's land came to his bounded white oak tree standing in a branch and further saith not. Given under our hands and seals this August 20, 1757, Charles Beaven, Robert Bradley, Joseph Sim

Robert Mills aged about 60 years being sworn at a ridge in a sunken place about half a mile or more to the north west of Mr. Calvert's now dwelling house and in a small thicket of trees declares that about 29-30 years ago when Mr. Darnall, deceased laid off a parcel of land for Mr. Hyde, this deponent carried the chain on said survey. He remembers that they run from Piscattaway Branch to a black oak which they bounded standing at or near the place above described and that he remembers they came there several times to the tree to lay off the land and further saith not. Given under our hands and seals this August 20, 1757, Robert Mills, Robert Bradley, Joseph Sim

Henry Darnall, Esqr., aged about 53 years, being sworn at a bounded white oak standing near the low ground of Piscattaway Branch opposite to Darnall's dwelling house and to the east side of the house and Piscattaway Branch, declares that on surveying the lands sold by Henry Darnall, Esqr., deceased (his father) to John Hyde he remembers when they came a little on the side of Mrs. Jane Brooke's plantation then in possession of Mr. Clement Brooke, deceased, they came to Piscattaway Main Branch and that they ran with the branch until they came to the white oak above described which they bounded and he further saith he well remembers they included all he lands then deemed to be held by Henry Darnall, Esqr., deceased (his father) that lay adjoining to Clement Brooke's, deceased his plantation and further saith not. Given under our hands and seals this August 20, 1757, Henry Darnall, Robert Bradley, Joseph Sim

Robert Mills aged about 60 years, being at the aforesaid white oak, declares that he carried the chain on the land sold by Henry Darnall, Esqr., deceased to John Hyde. He remembers that when they came to Piscattaway Main Branch on this side of Mrs. Jane

36

Brooke's plantation they run with said branch until they came in sight of Henry Darnall, Esqr., his house and on the east side of Piscattaway Branch and then they left off for that night and further saith not. Given under our hands and seals this August 20, 1757, Robert Mills, Robert Bradley, Joseph Sim

Charles Beaven aged about 60 years being sworn at a large bounded white oak standing on the right hand side of the road that leads from Mr. Ignatius Digges to Upper Marlborough Town and about 110 or 112 yards distance to the south west of said road, declares that about 30 years ago on a survey made for Mr. Hyde by Walter Hoxton on a parcel of land sold by him by Henry Darnall, Esqr., deceased, he remembers on running out the land they run with this deponent's land and also with the land held by Richard Keene, deceased and came to the aforesaid bounded white oak which he understood was a bounded tree of Darnall's land and that they run from thence near the forks of the road that leads to the Wood Yard and Bladensburg and further saith not. Given under our hands and seals this August 20, 1757, Charles Beaven, Robert Bradley, Joseph Sim

September 12, 1757, The deposition of Helena Collard aged about 50 years being first sworn at black oak standing near Charles Branch as described in Robert Mills deposition declares she remembers whenever the land was to be runout she understood they must begin at the black oak standing near Charles Branch, that she has often heard her husband Arnold Livers, deceased, say his land run with the branch falling into Charles Branch and that he claimed no lands on the other side of said branch and further saith not. Helena Collard, Robert Bradley, Joseph Sim

Benjamin Becraft aged about 48 years being first sworn at black oak standing near Charles Branch as described in Robert Mills deposition declares that about 12-13 years ago he lived on the plantation then in possession of Mr. Hyde as an overseer, that he remembers the land was several time run for Mr. Hyde at the request of Mr. Mattingly and Mr. Massey and that they had always begun at the said tree and he always understood it to be the beginning tree of Mr. Hyde's land and during the time of his living on said land he in company with Mr. Hyde Hoxton, Mr. Charles Beaven and several others came to the tree in order to shew Mr. Massey the tree. He believes they never finished surveying the land as he understood there was some mistake in the courses and well remembers in all the surveys left out land adjoining to Mrs. Jane Brooke and further saith that he was present when Mr. Calvert begun at said tree and he run into Mr. Ignatius Digges plantation and took in his houses and afterward run into Mr. Keene's old plantation he then left off, believing himself to be wrong as this deponent understood he not being constantly with them and further saith not. Given under our hands and seals this August 12, 1757, Benjamin Becraft, Robert Bradley, Joseph Sim

October 29, 1757; Henry Darnall, Esqr., being sworn at Mr. Benjamin Brooke, further saith that the survey made on the land mentioned in his other deposition, he believes was some time before the conveyance made from Henry Darnall, Esqr., deceased (his father) and that he believes there is but one boundary mentioned in said conveyance which is the beginning tree of said line and that he has understood that all the surveys since made by Mr. Hyde's managers and for Mr. Calvert have always left out some lands toward Mrs. Jane Brooke and that this deponent supposes the said land was run out by this deponents father and Mr. Walter Hoxton, Mr. Hyde's agent in order to ascertain the quantity of lands sold by his father and afterwards conveyed by him to Mr. John Hyde and further saith not. Henry Darnall, Robert Bradley, Joseph Sim

Page 60. At the request of Notley Jones the following Land Commission was recorded abt November 14, 1757

Memorandum that on the special petition of Notley Jones preferred to the justices of Prince George's County, Maryland on the 4th Tuesday in June in the 7th year of his Lordship commission the Right Hon. the Lord Proprietary Dominion etc., his Lordship commission issued by order of the justices aforesaid out of the county aforesaid on the 30th day of June Anno Domini 1757. In these words following, Frederick Absolute Lord and Proprietary of the Province of Maryland and

Avalon Lord Baron of Baltimore vizt; to Messrs George Fraser, Jonathan Burch, William Marbury and John Marlow of PGCo Gentleman, whereas Notley Jones, is seized of a tract called "Lyons Hole" and preferred his petition in writing to our county court held at Upper Marlborough Town before Peter Dent, Gentleman and his associates then and still justices within our county to examine evidence to prove and perpetuate the memory of the bounds of the said tract of land. Therefore, we command you any three or two of you to examine all witnesses or persons concerned touching their knowledge of the bounds of the said tract. Witness John Contee, Gentleman, June 30, 1757. Issued July 7, 1757, Joseph Sim, Clk

By virtue of a commission to examine evidences to prove the bounds of "Lyons Hole" we hereby give notice that we intend to meet at the lands on the 22nd instant. Witness our hands and seals this August 2, 1757, William Marbury, John Marlow

To the first, being now in the woods near the plantation of Notley Jones;

Edward Stonestreet, aged 53 or thereabouts, declares that about 30 years ago Mr. Richard Wade showed him the tree he now has his hand on and told him it was the bound tree between him and Mr. John Jones and further saith not.

Robert Wade, aged 53 or thereabouts, declares about 40 years ago Mr. John Jones showed this deponent white oak and said it was his beginning tree and it stood within 15 yards of the place he now stands and much about the same time Mr. William Penson showed this deponent the same tree and told him it was the beginning tree of Mr. John Jones who then lived on it and further saith not. To the Second {Boundary};

Robert Wade, aged 53 or thereabouts, declares about 36 years ago Mr. James Stoddert run from this place where he now stands or within 10 yards and at the same time Mr. John Jones, Mr. William Penson and Col. Thomas Addison told him that it was Mr. John Jones second tree and further saith not.

To the third {Boundary}

Robert Wade, aged 53 or thereabouts, declares about 40 years ago John Luis [sic Lewis] proved that Mr. Goodrick's bound tree stood within 10 yards of the place he now stands and further saith not.

John Lanham aged 68 years, declares that about 18 years ago he was shown this place where he now stands on or within 10 yards that there was a post set up and it was allowed to be a tree of Mr. John Jones land called "Lyons Hole" and further saith not.

William Lanham aged 39 years, declares that about 18 years ago there was a post standing up within 10 yards of the place he now stands and further saith not.

John Parnham, aged 48 or thereabouts, declares that about 8 years ago Henry Dickeson came within 40 yards of the place he now stands and showed this deponent a small maple and told him a bounded post of Mr. Goodrick's land and that it was the 3rd tree and further saith that about two years ago John Clark came with him to where he now stands and told him there stood the bounded post of Phillip Giddin's land [sic Gittings] and further saith not. To the fourth {Boundary}

Robert Wade, aged 53 or thereabouts, declares about 40 years ago Mr. John Jones showed him a bound tree that stood within 10 yards of where he now stands and thinks the tree he now has his hand on is the tree, and that it was his last bound tree and further saith not. William Marbury, John Marlow.

Page 63. At the request of John Moore the following Land Commission was recorded abt November 14, 1757

Memorandum that on the special petition of John Moore preferred to the justices of Prince George's County, Maryland on the 4th Tuesday in August in the 3rd year of his Lordship commission the Right Hon. the Lord Proprietary Dominion etc., his Lordship commission issued by order of the justices aforesaid out of the county aforesaid on the 31st day of August Anno Domini 1753. In these words following, Frederick Absolute Lord and Proprietary of the Province of Maryland and Avalon Lord Baron of Baltimore vizt; to Messrs Francis King, Luke Marbury, John Dunn and Robert Wade of PGCo Gentleman, whereas John Moore, is seized of part of a tract called "The Strife" and preferred his petition in writing to our county court held at Upper Marlborough Town before Peter Dent, Gentleman and his associates then and still justices within our county to

40

examine evidence to prove and perpetuate the memory of the bounds of the said tract of land. Therefore, we command you any three or two of you to examine all witnesses or persons concerned touching their knowledge of the bounds of the said tract. Witness Henry Truman, Gentleman, August 31, 1753. Issued August 31, 1753, Joseph Sim, Clk

Advertisement by virtue of a commission to examine evidences to prove the bounds of "The Strife" we hereby give notice that we intend to meet at the lands on Saturday, 22nd next month.. Witness our hands and seals this September 27, 1757, Luke Marbury, Robert Wade

October 22, 1757, depositions taken on the land, it being on the north side of Mattawoman Main Branch and near the main road that leads from Piscattaway to Zachia or Portobacco at a locust post and a large stone

Giles Vermillion aged 75 years or thereabouts declares that sixty years ago and sundry times since James Green, deceased, showed him a bounded Spanish oak tree where now stands a locust post and a large stone to be the first bounded tree of a tract called "Ayr" at that time but since called "Aix" which also he said was the first bounded tree of a tract called "The Strife"

Terrence O'Brian aged 78 years or thereabouts declares James Green showed him a bounded Spanish oak tree where now stands a locust post and a large stone and a marked hickory within 4 or 5 foot of the same to be the beginning tree of his two tracts of land.

John Harris, Jr. aged 67 years or thereabouts declares that his father John Harris, deceased, told him that the place where now stands a locust post and a large stone stood a boundary of James Green's land and that James Smallwood, deceased told him the same and that he had seen Mr. Thomas Marshall begin at the aforesaid place to run out a tract of land called "The Strife" and he saw and heard Mr. Francis Wheeler, deceased prove the said place to be the beginning of James Green's land before the commissioners that were then appointed.

Francis Burch aged 63 years or thereabouts declares his father John Burch, deceased, showed him a bounded Spanish oak where now stands a locust post and a large stone and told him the oak was the beginning tree of John Thompson's land and a bounded tree of James Green's land.

William Thompson aged 50 or thereabouts declares that about 28 years ago James Green, deceased showed him the stump of a tree with a large stone lying in it near to which stone stands a marked hickory and told him it was the beginning of two tracts of land called "Aix" and "The Strife."

John Thompson aged 26 years or thereabouts declares that about 8 years ago his father William Thompson, deceased showed him a post standing in the ground with a large stone lying near to which stands a marked hickory and told him the post and stone was in the same place where stood the beginning of two tracts of land called "Aix" and "The Strife." We went thence to a small branch commonly called Hinson's Branch [sic Hyne's Branch] and on the east side thereof and near a marked white oak we took the following depositions

Giles Vermillion, aged as before, declares that above 40 years ago he and George Dixon, deceased, were together at a bounded beech tree which stood in the said Hinds's Branch [sic Hyne's Branch] when Dixon told him that the beech tree was the last bound tree of "The Strife" and at the same time Dixon said there was a bound red oak to the said land standing lower down the branch. Dixon told him that he was informed of what he just said by Henry Robbins before this deponent made any purchase of land from Colonel Addison.

Robert Gordon, Sr., aged 65 years, declares he was informed that a beech tree stood in Hinson's Branch [sic Hyne's Branch] near to the place that now stands a marked white oak was the boundary of two tracts of land called "The Strife" and "Whitehaven" and that James Green, deceased, informed him that the land called "The Strife" went to Hinds's Branch [sic Hyne's Branch] and that he saw Mr. George Noble in running some lands for Colonel Addison beginning at the said beech which then was allowed to be a bound tree of "The Strife" and run from thence down the branch to Mattawoman.

Oliver Harris aged 77 years declares that he was with Mr. Peter Dent, deceased when he was running a tract called "Whitehaven" and he told this deponent that a beach tree which stood in Hinds's Branch [sic Hyne's Branch] within 3 or 4 foot stands a marked white oak was the second bound tree of "Whitehaven." We went from thence to a bounded red oak near to north side of Mattawoman

Terrence O'Brian aged as before declares about 50 odd years ago Major Dent deceased showed and told him the red oak was his first boundary of a tract called "Whitehaven" then in his possession by which red oak went an Indian path. This deponent further saith that George Dixon, deceased told him the red oak was the last bound tree of his land, "Dixon's."

John Harris, Sr. aged 67 declares he saw the red oak proved by Terrence O'Brian to be the first bound tree of "Whitehaven" and that he knew an old Indian path that went close by.

Joseph Evans aged 39 years or thereabouts declares that about 12-13 years ago George Dixon, deceased was with this deponent looking for timber and they came to the spot where he now stands where formerly stood a beech tree as told by the said Dixon to be the second line tree of "Whitehaven"

Joseph Evans aged as before declares that about 12-13 years ago George Dixon, deceased and this deponent were at work together near a red oak and that some person was trimming the tree and when he asked Dixon for what purpose that was done, Dixon said the oak tree was a beginning tree of Mr. Peter Dent's land called "Whitehaven" and the last bounded tree of "The Strife." Luke Marbury, Robert Wade

{mm, There were two tracts in PGCo both named "The Strife" and "Whitehaven"}

Early Landowners of Maryland, by Robert W. Hall
Volume 2: Prince George's County
1650-1710
Volume 4: Charles County
1640-1710

"The Strife"
11/10/1695 — 1,302a's. C3i/99 SR7377
Location: PISC/RR on the north side of Mattawoman Creek on a small branch by an Indian path near the east side of a great

branch beginning at the first bound tree of Thomas Trethrick's tract of land called "Ayr." Also adjoins William Dent's tract called "Whitehaven"
Other persons mentioned: William Dent (assignor of land rights).

"Whitehaven" 11/10/1695 — 890a's. C3i/109 SR7377
Location: PISC adjoining a tract called "The Strife" and Robert Wade's land called "Forrest Green." In the woods on the north side of Mattawoman (aka St. Thomas) Creek beginning at the last bound tree of John Addison and William Hutchison's tract of land called "The Strife." Also adjoins Robert Wade's tract called "Stoney Harbor Resurveyed"
Other persons mentioned: William Hutchison (assignor of land rights

Page 66. At the request of Thomas Boyd the following Land Commission was recorded abt November 14, 1757
Memorandum that on the special petition of Thomas Boyd preferred to the justices of Prince George's County, Maryland on the 4th Tuesday in June in the 7th year of his Lordship commission the Right Hon. the Lord Proprietary Dominion etc., his Lordship commission issued by order of the justices aforesaid out of the county aforesaid on the 7th day of July Anno Domini 1757. In these words following, Frederick Absolute Lord and Proprietary of the Province of Maryland and Avalon Lord Baron of Baltimore vizt; to Messrs Mordecai Jacob, Thomas Williams, Robert Tyler and Jeremiah Belt, Jr., of PGCo Gentleman, whereas Thomas Boyd, is seized of a tract called "The Forrest" and preferred his petition in writing to our county court held at Upper Marlborough Town before Peter Dent, Gentleman and his associates then and still justices within our county to examine evidence to prove and perpetuate the memory of the bounds of the said tract of land. Therefore, we command you any three or two of you to examine all witnesses or persons concerned touching their knowledge of the bounds of the said tract. Witness John Contee, Gentleman, June 30, 1757. Issued July 7, 1757, Joseph Sim, Clk
Pursuant to a commission to examine evidences to prove the

bounds of "The Forrest" we hereby give notice that we intend to meet at the dwelling house of Rachel Boyd on Monday, November 14th next. Witness our hands and seals this October 3, 1757, Mordecai Jacob, Thomas Williams, Jeremiah Belt, Jr.

On November 14, 1757 we met and proceeded to a marked white oak standing about 25 yards to the southward of the late Richard Jones plantation

Samuel Waters aged 51 years or thereabouts, Quaker, affirmed that about 28 years ago he was shown this tree by Thomas Swearingen as a corner tree of "The Forrest" then in possession of said Swearingen. Then we proceeded to a bounded hickory standing about 200 yards to the north east of the late Samuel Davis dwelling house where the said Waters affirmed that about 20 years ago Samuel Davis brought him to this place to run the first line of a tract that Davis bought of Thomas Swearingen and that he run a south course about 120 perches and that he believes the hickory to be the tree he ran from. Jeremiah Belt, Jr., Mordecai Jacob, Thomas Williams

Page 68. At the request of William Newman Dorsett the following Land Commission was recorded abt November 14, 1757

Memorandum that on the special petition of William Newman Dorsett preferred to the justices of Prince George's County, Maryland on the 4th Tuesday in June in the 7th year of his Lordship commission the Right Hon. the Lord Proprietary Dominion etc., his Lordship commission issued by order of the justices aforesaid out of the county aforesaid on the 7th day of July Anno Domini 1757. In these words following, Frederick Absolute Lord and Proprietary of the Province of Maryland and Avalon Lord Baron of Baltimore vizt; to Messrs William Eversfield, Daniel Page, Thomas Hodgkin and William Deakins of PGCo Gentleman, whereas William Newman Dorsett, is seized of a tract called "Calvert's Manor" and preferred his petition in writing to our county court held at Upper Marlborough Town before Peter Dent, Gentleman and his associates then and still justices within our county to examine evidence to prove and perpetuate the memory of the bounds of the said tract of land. Therefore, we command you any three or two of you to examine all witnesses or persons concerned touching their knowledge of the bounds of the said tract. Witness John Contee, Gentleman, June 30, 1757. Issued July 7, 1757, Joseph Sim, Clk

Advertisement, by virtue of a commission to examine evidences to prove the bounds of "Calvert's Manor" we hereby give notice that we intend to meet at the lands on Monday, June 29th instant Witness our hands and seals this May 14, 1757, William Eversfield, William Deakins, Thomas Hodgkin

Aaron Orme aged 62 years or thereabouts declares about 18 years ago William Groome, deceased told him that a black oak tree that stood on the south side of a hill where now is placed a large stone and within 200 yards of Mr. William Bowie's dwelling house was a bounded tree of said Groome's father Richard Groome's land and further saith not. Aaron Orme, William Eversfield, William Deakins, Thomas Hodgkin

Thomas King aged 51-1/2 years or thereabouts declares that about 30 years ago Richard Groome, deceased told him that a black oak tree that stood on the south side of a hill where now is placed a large stone and within 200 yards of Mr. William Bowie's dwelling house was a bounded tree of said Groome's land and further saith not. Thomas King, William Eversfield, William Deakins, Thomas Hodgkin

Page 69. At the request of Jeremiah Crabb the following Supersedes was recorded November 22, 1757

You Jeremiah Crabb, Edward Crabb and John McGill do confess judgment to Samuel Galloway for the sum of 25 pounds 8 shillings and 8 pence sterling, 278 pounds tobacco and 6 pence currency which sums were recovered on the fourth Tuesday of August last to be levied on your goods chattels lands or tenements for the use of Samuel Galloway in case Jeremiah Crabb shall not pay and satisfy the said sum and costs thereon on February 10th next. November 19, 1757, Mordecai Jacob, Robert Tyler

Page 70. At the request of Francis Piles, Sr. the following

Supersedes was recorded November 22, 1757

You Francis Piles, Sr., Henry Darnall and Timothy Drew do confess judgment to Joseph Adams for the sum of 1 pound 19 shillings and 7 pence current money which sum was recovered on August 18, 1757 before me one of His Lordships Justices of the Peace to be levied on your goods chattels lands or tenements for the use of Joseph Adams in case Francis Piles, Sr. shall not pay and satisfy the said sum and costs thereon on February 10th next. George Gordon

Page 70. At the request of Benjamin Talbott the following Certificate of Stray was recorded November 22, 1757

PGCo Sct, October 7, 1757; I hereby certify that Benjamin Talbott brought before me a black horse as a stray that has been troublesome for the past two years. Is about 13 hands high, branded on the shoulder and buttock, docked and broke to the saddle. George Gordon

Page 70. At the request of William Mahew the following Certificate of Stray was recorded November 22, 1757

PGCo Sct, November 19, 1757; I hereby certify that William Mahew brought before me an iron grey mare taken up as a stray, about 12-13 hands high, branded imperfectly on both buttocks and 7-8 years old. Joseph Belt, Jr.

Page 70. At the request of John Brashear, Sr. the following Supersedes was recorded November 22, 1757

You John Brashear, Sr., Andrew Seymour and Isaac Brashear do confess judgment to Rebecca Tilley for the sum of 11 pounds 15 shillings and 11 pence sterling, 40 pounds 12 shillings and 11 pence currency and 60-3/4 pounds tobacco which sums were recovered on the fourth Tuesday of August last to be levied on your goods chattels lands or tenements for the use of Rebecca Tilley in case John Brashear, Sr. shall not pay and satisfy the said sum and costs thereon on February 10th next. November 22, 1757, John Hepburn

Page 71. At the request of Thomas Cramphin the following

Mortgage was recorded November 23, 1757
Indenture made October 26, 1757; Barton Lucas in consideration of 59 pounds current money of Maryland paid by Thomas Cramphin has sold part of a tract called "Hop Yard" willed to the said Barton Lucas by his father Thomas Lucas on May 31, 1756 and containing 138 acres, provided that if Barton Lucas shall well and truly pay unto Thomas Cramphin the aforesaid sum of money on or before the expiration of three years from the date of these presents then this obligation to be void. Signed Barton Lucas in the presence of and acknowledged before John Cooke, Christopher Lowndes

Page 72. At the request of John Baynes the following Deed was recorded November 23, 1757
Indenture made October 11, 1757; between Thomas Boteler, Gentleman and John Baynes, Gentleman. Witnesseth that whereas Henry Boteler (father of Thomas Boteler) was seized in his demesne in part of a tract called "Appledore" containing 242 acres as by deed of conveyance from John Middleton to Henry Boteler bearing date July 9, 1709. That by the death of Henry Boteler the part of land descended to the said Thomas Boteler, that by the lines of an elder tract of land called "Wheelers Hope" being lately extended to some reputed bounds, so much of the land is therein included that there appears to remain clear of the said "Wheelers Hope" 135 acres of the 242 acres part of "Appledore" above mentioned. This Indenture therefore further witnesseth that Thomas Boteler in consideration of 30 pounds current money paid by John Baynes has sold part of "Appledore" now containing 135 acres. Signed Thomas Boteler in the presence of John Hepburn, David Ross and acknowledged before John Hepburn

Page 74. At the request of Richard Mason the following Certificate of Stray was recorded November 29, 1757
November 28, 1757; This is to certify that Richard Mason brought before me as a stray a small bay horse about 12 hands high, branded on the near thigh and the off shoulder, whitish splotch for a scald or the rubbing of traces. Nathaniel Magruder

Page 74. At the request of John Ryon the following Certificate of Stray was recorded November 30, 1757
PGCo Sct, November 20, 1757; This is to certify that John Ryon brought before me as a stray a small black mare, branded on the near shoulder, she has a young colt. Nathaniel Magruder

Page 74. At the request of John Sissell, Jr. the following Certificate of Stray was recorded December 12, 1757
PGCo Sct, December 8, 1757; John Sissell, Jr., brought before me a small black mare, 12 hands high, a small star in her forehead, branded on the near buttock and says she is troublesome and breaks into his inclosures. Christopher Lowndes

Page 74. At the request of Thomas Waring the following Certificate of Stray was recorded December 12, 1757
PGCo Sct, December 10, 1757; I hereby certify that Mr. Thomas Waring sent before me a mealy bay horse taken up as a stray about 13 hands high appears very old, has some saddle spots, an appearance of a brand on both his shoulders, paces and gallops. John Cooke

Page 75. At the request of John Higgins the following Deed was recorded December 14, 1757
Indenture made November 30, 1757; Samuel Lucas, farmer of Frederick County, Maryland in consideration of 55 pounds current money paid by John Higgins, tailor of PGCo has sold one moiety of part of a tract called "Evans Range" being that part of 200 acres made over by deed of gift by Elizabeth Lucas his mother on December 20, 1744 and recorded into Liber BB Folio 245. Signed Samuel Lucas in the presence of and acknowledged before John Cooke, Thomas Williams and at the same time Elizabeth Lucas wife of Samuel Lucas relinguished her right of dower

Page 76. At the request of Gilbert Sprigg the following Release was recorded December 16, 1757
I Enoch Magruder, merchant have received this present day of Gilbert Sprigg, planter the sums of 76 pounds 6 shillings and 6

pence sterling money of Great Britain and 10 pounds 2 shillings current money being in full for the redemption of the following Negroes; Sharper, Peg, Sall and Nacey. Also 1 black horse, 1 grey mare and colt, 5 cows, 2 calves and 3 yearlings specified in indenture bearing date October 15, 1756. In witness whereof I have hereunto set my hand and seal this December 7, 1757, Enoch Magruder in the presence of Thomas Williams

Page 76. At the request of Clement Trigg, Jr. the following Certificate of Stray was recorded December 24, 1757
PGCo Sct, December 23, 1757; Clement Trigg, Jr. brought before me a small dark bay mare, a star in her forehead, 1 white foot, has no visible brand and with her is a small colt of a dark bay color. Christopher Lowndes

Page 77. At the request of William Linton the following Supersedes was recorded December 28, 1757
You William Linton, Thomas Harwood and Thomas Pindell do confess judgment to Turnor Wootton for the sums of 37 pounds of tobacco and 6 pence currency which sums were recovered this day before me one of His Lordships Justices of the Peace to be levied on your goods chattels lands or tenements for the use of Turnor Wootton in case William Linton shall not pay and satisfy the said sum and costs thereon on February 10th next. November 10, 1757, Robert Tyler

Page 78. At the request of Charles Hodges the following Deed was recorded December 31, 1757
Indenture made August 8, 1757; Edward Digges, planter in consideration of 31 pounds 7 shillings sterling paid by Charles Hodges, planter has sold part of three tracts called "Scott's Lot," "Hugh's Labor" and "Riley's Folly" beginning at "Brock Hall" and containing 78-1/2 acres. Signed Edward Digges in the presence of and acknowledged before John Cooke, Nathaniel Magruder and at the same time Mary Digges wife of Edward Digges relinguished her right of dower

Page 78. At the request of Jasper Manduit the following Deed was recorded December 31, 1757

Indenture made December 21, 1757; John Halsall, heir, executor and administrator of William Renshaw {d. 1742}, planter in consideration of 40 pounds current money paid by Jasper Manduit has sold a tract called "Cuckolds Delight" containing 100 acres and beginning at Loyles Branch. Signed John Halsall in the presence of and acknowledged before David Ross, Christopher Lowndes and at the same time Pretious Halsall wife of John Halsall relinguished her right of dower

Page 80. At the request of Thomas Allen the following Mortgage was recorded January 4, 1758

Indenture made December 5, 1758; Samuel Carnole, weaver in consideration of 1800 pounds of tobacco paid by Thomas Allen, planter has sold part of "Beall's Purchase" containing 64 acres and lying on the beaver dams near Bladensburg. Also 1 dark bay horse, 1 bay mare, 1 bright bay mare and 1 grey mare provided nevertheless that Samuel Carnole do well and sufficiently bear harmless Thomas Allen from all debts which may occur by reason of an execution now served on Samuel Carnole by virtue of a judgment obtained by Christopher Lowndes & Company against him for 1600 pounds tobacco with legal costs or in case Samuel Carnole shall well and truly pay the quantity of tobacco before the 10th day of March next, then the above deed shall be void. Signed Samuel Carnole in the presence of John Hepburn, Edward Clagett and acknowledged before John Hepburn

Page 81. At the request of Thomas Cramphin the following Deed was recorded January 7, 1758

Indenture made January 5, 1758; John Beall son of John, house carpenter, in consideration of 7 pound 17 shillings and 6 pence sterling money paid by Thomas Cramphin has sold a tract called "Coll {Cool} Spring" being part of "New Dumfrize" taken up by Mr. John Beall, Sr., containing 15 acres and beginning in the third line of "Yarrow" formerly in possession of Joseph Chew. Signed John Beall son of John in the presence of and acknowledged before John Hepburn and at the same time Mary Beall wife of John Beall relinguished her right of dower {now

51

lies in Washington DC}

Page 83.   At the request of Walter Williams the following
Certificate of Stray was recorded January 7, 1758
PGCo Sct, January 3, 1758; Mr. Walter Williams brought before
me as a trespasser and stray a bright bay horse branded on the
near shoulder and buttock, his near hind foot white, a blaze in
his face, snip on his nose, trimmed with a standing mane, shoed
on his fore feet, his tail bobbed. Mordecai Jacob.

Page 83.   At the request of William Neall the following
Supersedes was recorded January 9, 1758
You William Neall, Thomas Selby and James Sasser do confess
judgment to Mark Webb for the sums of 2 pound 10 shillings
debt and 2 shillings and 6 pence currency costs and 20 shillings
and 2 pence currency debt and 2 shillings and 6 pence currency
costs which sums were recovered on October 1, 1757 before me
one of His Lordships Justices of the Peace to be levied on your
goods chattels lands or tenements for the use of Mark Webb in
case William Neall shall not pay and satisfy the said sum and
costs thereon on February 10th next. Thomas Contee

Page 83. At the request of James Pelly the following Supersedes
was recorded January 9, 1758
You James Pelly, James Harvey and James Sasser do confess
judgment to Bernard Lynch for the sums of 10 shillings
currency debt and 2 shillings and 6 pence costs and 20 shillings
which sums were recovered on September 23, 1757 before me
one of His Lordships Justices of the Peace to be levied on your
goods chattels lands or tenements for the use of Bernard Lynch
in case James Pelly shall not pay and satisfy the said sum and
costs thereon on February 10th next. Thomas Contee

Page 83. At the request of Shadrack Casteel the following Deed
of Gift was recorded January 13, 1758
Indenture made January 13, 1758; Rachel Watkins in
consideration of all proper necessities of life found and
provided for me during my natural life and the love good will

52

and affection that she hath and bear unto her loving cousin Shadrack Casteel also for divers other causes and considerations her hereunto moving have given him by these presents, 2 beds, 2 blankets, 2 sheets, 2 rugs, 1 quilt, 2 bolsters, 2 pillows, 2 pillow cases, 4 sows, 28 pigs, 5 barrows, 2 iron pots, 6 dishes, 6 plates, 2 dozen spoons, 1 chest with 20 yards of fine linen, 2 yards of black silk, 6 yards of striped Holland, 3 yards of red shalloon, 1 pair of women's shoes, 2 pair of children shoes and stockings, 1 child's hat, 15 barrels of Indian corn, 1 frying pan, 1 sifter, 2 hoes, 1 ax, 1 plough, 2 chisels, 1 pruning knife, 1 hatchet, 1 hammer, 1 man's coat, 1 man's jacket, 1 pair of man's breeches, 1 pair of man's shoes, 1 pair of men's stockings, 1 spinning wheel, 1 woolen wheel, 1 pair of wool cards, 6 tea cups, 1 gold ring, 1 man's saddle, 1 bridle, 1 horse, 3 basons, 1 bag, parcel of flax, 1 skillet, 1 chamber pot, 2 bedstead, 1 lock, also pins and needles and sundry other things in the abovementioned chest. Signed Rachel Watkins, in the presence of George Gordon, Mary Watson and acknowledged before George Gordon

Page 84. At the request of William Beall, Jr. the following Deed was recorded January 14, 1758
Indenture made January 12, 1758; Daniel Carroll of Frederick County, Maryland, Gentleman in consideration of 100 pounds currency paid by William Beall, Jr., planter has sold two adjacent tracts of land called "Batchelors Choice" containing 100 acres and "Batchelors Content" containing 176 acres lying on the east side of the East Paint Branch of Eastern Branch of Potomack River. Signed Daniel Carroll, in the presence of John Hepburn, Charles Carroll, Jr., and acknowledged before John Hepburn and at the same time Eleanor Carroll wife of Daniel Carroll relinguished her right of dower

Page 86. At the request of Samuel White the following Certificate of Stray was recorded January 14, 1758
PGCo Sct; I hereby certify that Samuel White brought before me a roanish bay colored horse taken up as a stray, 14 hands high, no brand, appears to have been ploughed or drawn. January 13,

1758, Robert Tyler

Page 86. At the request of Zachariah Lyles the following Indenture was recorded January 17, 1758
Indenture made January 9, 1758; John Cross in consideration of 35 pounds currency paid by Zachariah Lyles has covenanted and agreed by these presents that John Cross shall well and truly serve him as his servant during the term of 5 years. Signed John Cross, Zachariah Lyles and acknowledged before Robert Tyler

Page 87. At the request of Richard Snowden the following Bill of Sale was recorded January 20, 1758
I Thomas Hobson, planter in consideration of 75 pounds 17 shillings and 4 pence current money now due and owing to Richard Snowden, iron master of Anne Arundel County, Maryland do sell two servant men named James Butleblunt and William Williams together with 1 young horse, 2 mares, 2 cows and calves, 2 sows and pigs and all my crop of tobacco, household goods and other implements whatsoever. In witness whereof I have hereunto set my hand and seal this January 16, 1758, Thomas Hobson in the presence of Samuel Snowden, Evan Thomas and acknowledged before Mordecai Jacob

Page 88. At the request of Francis Hall the following Mortgage was recorded January 21, 1758
Indenture made November 8, 1757; Samuel Pottinger and Eleanor Pottinger his wife, planters in consideration of 52 pounds 11 shillings sterling paid by Francis Hall, Gentleman have sold several tracts laid out in "Major's Lott" formerly taken up by Colonel Ninian Beall containing 180 acres provided that if Samuel Pottinger shall well and truly pay unto Francis Hall the aforesaid sum of money with legal interest at or upon the 10th day of November 1758, then this indenture to be void. Signed Samuel Pottinger, Eleanor Pottinger in the presence of and acknowledged before Thomas Williams, Robert Tyler

Page 89. At the request of George Noble the following Deed was recorded January 30, 1758

Indenture made December 16, 1757; between William Hicks of St. Mary's County, Maryland, merchant and George Noble, planter of PGCo. Witnesseth that whereas George Noble has a penal bond of William Hicks for the conveying and making over unto the said George Noble all the right title and interest of William Hicks and also all the right title and interest whereof John Hicks (father of said William) died seized of. This indenture therefor further witnesseth that William Hicks for the consideration above expressed as also for divers other good causes him hereunto moving has sold unto George Noble part of a tract formerly granted to William Calvert commonly called "Piscattaway Manor" (otherwise "Calvert's Manor" alias "Elizabeth Manor") lying on Piscattaway Creek and now in possession of George Noble. Beginning at the end of the 18th course of 600 acres in the possession of Thomas Noble and George Noble. Containing 46 acres and binding on a line of Thomas Noble's division expressed in a deed of partition between Thomas Noble, George Noble, Zachariah Wade and Anne Wade his wife. Signed William Hicks, in the presence of James Biscoe, Basil Biscoe and acknowledged before James Biscoe, William Hebb, JP's of St. Mary's County, Maryland and at the same time Priscilla Hicks wife of William Hicks relinguished her right of dower

Page 91. At the request of George Noble the following Deed was recorded January 30, 1758

Indenture made December 16, 1757; William Hicks of St. Mary's County, Maryland, merchant in consideration of 25,110 pounds of crop tobacco paid by George Noble, planter has sold part of a tract formerly granted to William Calvert commonly called "Piscattaway Manor" (otherwise "Calvert's Manor" alias "Elizabeth Manor") lying on Piscattaway Creek and now in possession of George Noble. Beginning on the 21st line of 600 acres in the possession of Thomas Noble and George Noble and containing 186 acres and binding on a line of George Noble's division expressed in a deed of partition between George Noble, Thomas Noble, Zachariah Wade and Anne Wade his wife, the west line of the 1000 acres of land George Noble (father of said George Noble) purchased of Thomas Edelen, and Piscattaway Creek. Signed William Hicks, in the presence of James Biscoe, Basil Biscoe and acknowledged before James Biscoe, William Hebb, JP's of St. Mary's County, Maryland and at the same time Priscilla Hicks wife of William Hicks relinguished her right of dower

Page 92. At the request of Mary Young the following Certificate of Stray was recorded February 4, 1758
January 31, 1758, PGCo; This day was brought before me by Miss Molly Young and iron grey horse about 13 hands high, branded on ye near buttock. She complains he breaks into her inclosures. Christopher Lowndes

Page 93. At the request of Samuel Queen the following Bill of Sale was recorded February 4, 1758
I Barton Lucas in consideration of 70 pound 4 shillings and 3 pence Maryland currency and 10200 pounds of tobacco paid by Samuel Queen has sold four Negroes; Jeane, George, Amey and Simon, also 30 hogs, 3 cows and calves, 1 bed and furniture, 3 iron pots and 2 draft horses. In witness whereof I have set my hand and seal this January 30, 1758, Barton Lucas in the presence of Luke Windsor, Isaac Darnall

Page 93. At the request of Andrew Abington the following Deed of Gift was recorded February 7, 1758
Indenture made January 19, 1758; Mary Scott, Gentlewoman in consideration of 5 shillings as for the maternal love and affection she hath and doth bear to her son Andrew Abington doth give a tract called "Speedwell" said to contain 93 acres. Signed Mary Scott, in the presence of George Parker, John Dawson and acknowledged before George Gordon, Nathaniel Magruder

Page 94. At the request of Benjamin Higdon the following Deed was recorded February 11, 1758
Indenture made January 24, 1758; Samuel Biggs, planter of

PGCo, in consideration of 5000 pounds of tobacco paid by Benjamin Higdon, carpenter of Charles County, Maryland has sold a tract called "Radford's Chance" containing 190 acres and binding on Philip Tenaly's land. Signed Samuel Biggs in the presence of John Hepburn, George Clarke and acknowledged before John Hepburn

Page 95. At the request of Thomas Conner the following Certificate of Stray was recorded February 21, 1758
PGCo Sct, February 17, 1758; I hereby certify that Thomas Conner living on a plantation belonging to Benedict Calvert, Esqr., brought before me a young bay mare take up as a stray, unbroken, branded on the near buttock, undocked and appears to be 4 years old.

Page 96. At the request of Robert McClish the following Certificate of Stray was recorded March 1, 1758
PGCo Sct, February 27, 1758, I certify that Robert McClish brought before me as a trespasser and stray a small black mare branded on the off buttock, a star and snip and one white foot and she is a natural pacer, both ears cropt. Thomas Williams

Page 96. At the request of John Abington the following Deed was recorded March 4, 1758
Indenture made January 30, 1758; Philip Tennally, planter in consideration of 5 shillings current money of Maryland paid by John Abington, Gentleman, has sold a tract called "Speedwell" containing 138 acres being the plantation that Doctor Andrew Scott lived on and afterward the said Philip Tennally and now in possession of John Abington. To have and to hold the said tract unto John Abington for and during the natural life of Dr. Andrew Scott paying yearly unto Philip Tennally one pepper corn. Signed Philip Tennally in the presence of John Hepburn, Clement Hill and acknowledged before John Hepburn

Page 96. At the request of Benjamin Gittings the following Certificate of Stray was recorded March 4, 1758
PGCo Sct, March 2, 1758; I certify that Benjamin Gittings

brought before me as a trespassing stray a small brown horse, no brand, near hind food white and one cropped ear. Thomas Williams

Page 97. At the request of Zachariah Scott the following Certificate of Stray was recorded March 4, 1758
PGCo Sct, March 2, 1758; Zachariah Scott brought before me a black mare about 12 hands high, branded on the buttock, he complains she is troublesome and breaks into his inclosures. Christopher Lowndes

Page 97. At the request of Peter Brown the following Certificate of Stray was recorded March 10, 1758
PGCo Sct, March 7, 1758; Peter Brown brought before me a stray mare of a bright bay color with a bald face, no brand, about 12 hands high, he complains she is troublesome and breaks into his inclosures. Christopher Lowndes

Page 97. At the request of John Glassford & Company the following Bill of Sale was recorded March 11, 1758
I John Loggins, planter in consideration of 5000 pounds of crop tobacco and 10 pounds current money paid by John Glassford & Company have sold the following goods and chattels; a black horse, a gray horse, 9 cattle, 20 hogs, 10 sheep, 2 good feather beds with bedsteads and all furniture, 1 other feather bed not so good with furniture, 1 desk,1 oval table, 1 chest, 3 pewter dishes and 6 pewter plates, 2 pewter basons, 2 iron pots, 1 frying pan, 6 flag bottom chairs. In witness whereof I have set my hand and seal this March 10, 1758, John Loggins in the presence of George Gantt

Page 97. At the request of James Marshall the following Deed was recorded March 11, 1758
Indenture made March 11, 1758; Ralph Pickerell, merchant and Elizabeth Pickerell his wife in consideration of 5000 pounds of crop tobacco paid by James Marshall has sold parts of two tracts, one called "Chance" containing 100 acres and the other called "Addition to Chance" containing 15 acres and lying on the

west side of Patuxent River and north side of Mattawoman Swamp and beginning at James Gamblin's land. Signed Ralph Pickerell, Elizabeth Pickerell in the presence of John Hepburn, J. Sprigg and acknowledged before John Hepburn and at the same time Elizabeth Pickerell wife of Ralph Pickerell relinguished her right of dower

Page 98. At the request of George Hardey, Jr. the following Deed was recorded March 11, 1758
Indenture made February 22, 1758; Henry Hardey, Jr., planter and Sarah Hardey his wife in consideration of 100 pounds sterling of Great Britain paid by George Hardey has sold a tract called "Conveniency" containing 244 acres and beginning at a white oak standing by the main branch of Mattawoman being a bound tree of James Gambra's land. Also a tract called "Tyler's Advantage on Conveniency" containing 247 acres and beginning at a tract called "Conveniency" formerly belonging to Henry Massey, deceased. Signed Henry Hardey, Jr., Sarah Hardey in the presence of and acknowledged before George Gordon, George Gantt and at the same time Sarah Hardey wife of Henry Hardey, Jr., relinguished her right of dower

Page 100. At the request of Henry Hardey the following Deed was recorded March 11, 1758
Indenture made February 24, 1758; George Hardey, Jr., planter in consideration of 110 pounds sterling of Great Britain paid by Henry Hardey has sold a tract called "Conveniency" containing 244 acres and beginning at a white oak standing by the main branch of Mattawoman being a bound tree of James Gambra's land. Also a tract called "Tyler's Advantage on Conveniency" containing 247 acres and beginning at a tract called "Conveniency" formerly belonging to Henry Massey, deceased. Signed George Hardey, Jr., in the presence of and acknowledged before George Gordon, George Gantt and at the same time Lucy Hardey wife of George Hardey, Jr., relinguished her right of dower

Page 101. At the request of Alexander Falconar, Jr. the following

Bill of Sale was recorded March 4, 1758
I Alexander Falconar, Sr. in consideration of 28 pounds 6 shillings current money paid by my son Alexander Falconar, Jr. have sold the following goods and chattels, all ye tobacco now in my tobacco house, 2 black horses, 1 old bay mare, a sow and 4 pigs and a gilt and 14 shoates, 2 ewes. In witness whereof I have set my hand and seal this February 28, 1758, Alexander Falconar in the presence of Thomas McGill, John McGill

Page 102. At the request of James Lucas the following Certificate of Stray was recorded March 25, 1758
PGCo Sct, March 25, 1758; James Lucas (living on the south west branch of Patuxent River) brought before me a small mare take up as a stray, her color a mealy bay, is shod before, has a star in her forehead but no brand, 4 years old and paces. John Cooke

Page 102. At the request of John Moore the following Certificate of Stray was recorded March 28, 1758
I certify that this day John Moore brought before me a small brown mare as a trespasser and stray branded on the near buttock, a blaze face and four white feet, several saddle spots. Thomas Williams

Page 102. At the request of William Jenkins the following Certificate of Stray was recorded March 28, 1758
I certify that this day William Jenkins of Piscattaway Hundred brought before me a small dark bay horse, uncut, about 12 hands high, the off hind foot white, branded imperfectly, 4 years old. Joseph Belt, Jr.

Page 102. At the request of John Stone Hawkins the following Assignment of Mortgage was recorded March 29, 1758
Indenture made March 21, 1758; between Samuel Roundell, Gentleman and John Stone Hawkins, merchant. Whereas by one indenture bearing date November 26, 1755 between Hezekiah Magruder and Samuel Roundell the said Hezekiah Magruder in consideration of 136 pounds 19 shillings and 7 pence sterling money and 24 pounds 9 shillings current money of Maryland

did make over to Samuel Roundell three tracts of land called "New Exchange" containing 72 acres, "Quick Sale" containing 100 acres and "Anchovies Hills" containing 30 acres, the whole 202 acres and recorded in Liber NN, folio 407-408. Now this indenture witnesseth that Samuel Roundell in consideration of 92 pounds 18 shilling current money paid by John Stone Hawkins and diverse other good causes, the said Samuel Roundell thereunto moving have assigned the aforesaid three tracts of land. Signed Samuel Roundell in the presence of John Hepburn , J. Harrison and acknowledged before John Hepburn

Page 104. At the request of Mary Banicker the following Assignment was recorded March 31, 1758
I Mary Welsh received of Mary Banicker a full consideration for a Mulatto servant called Samuel Morter and I therefore have assigned over to Mary Banicker the said servant. Given under my hand and seal this February 27, 1758, Mary Welsh.
Test: James Crow

Page 104. At the request of Samuel Scott the following Land Commission was recorded abt March 31, 1758
Memorandum that on the special petition of Samuel Scott preferred to the justices of Prince George's County, Maryland on the 4th Tuesday in March in the 6th year of his Lordship commission the Right Hon. the Lord Proprietary Dominion etc., his Lordship commission issued by order of the justices aforesaid out of the county aforesaid on the 2nd day of April Anno Domini 1757. In these words following, Frederick Absolute Lord and Proprietary of the Province of Maryland and Avalon Lord Baron of Baltimore vizt; to Messrs James Beck, Richard Isaac, Jr., Lewis Duvall, Mordecai Jacob of PGCo Gentleman, whereas Samuel Scott, is seized of a tract called "Girls Portion" and preferred his petition in writing to our county court held at Upper Marlborough Town before Peter Dent, Gentleman and his associates then and still justices within our county to examine evidence to prove and perpetuate the memory of the bounds of the said tract of land. Therefore, we command you any three or two of you to examine all witnesses

or persons concerned touching their knowledge of the bounds of the said tract. Witness Joseph Belt, Jr., Gentleman, March 26, 1757. Issued April 2, 1757, Joseph Sim, Clk

In Obedience to the commission gave public notice and met at the dwelling house of Mr. Samuel Scott on August 20, 1757, when no evidence appearing we adjourned till October 8th next and proceeded to a bounded white oak standing on the Piney Branch of the Eastern Branch and south side of Potomack River Mr. William Hall aged about 41 years declared that about 16 years ago Thomas Johnson showed him the said white oak and told him it was the beginning tree of a tract called "Girls Portion" and further saith that he has known several people run from the said white oak as the beginning tree and further saith not.

Mr. Joseph Walker aged about 41 years declared that he has known several people run from the said white oak as the beginning tree of Thomas Scott's land and further saith not. James Beck, Mordecai Jacob

Page 106. At the request of William Watson the following Deed was recorded April 1, 1758
Indenture made March 29, 1758; James Watson, Sr., planter in consideration of 22 pounds sterling money of Great Britain paid by William Watson, Sr., part of two tracts called "Cole Brooke" formerly called "Poplar Hills" and "Watson's Forrest" containing 100 acres. Signed James Watson, in the presence of John Hepburn, Peregrine Mackaness for the sum of 1 pound 14 shillings and 6 pence debt and 10 shillings and 6 pence costs currency which sums were recovered on July 12, 1757 before me one of His Lordships Justices of the Peace to be levied on your goods chattels lands or tenements for the use of Peregrine Mackaness and acknowledged before John Hepburn [no wife release dower}

Page 107. At the request of John Miles the following Release was recorded April 5, 1758
PGCo Sct, April 5, 1757; I hereby release unto John Miles all my right title claim interest and demand unto the within mentioned mortgaged Negroes having received full satisfaction. Signed

Hancock Lee in the presence of Joseph Sim Thomas Brooke.
Note: Mortgage recorded in Liber NN folio 506.

Page 108. At the request of John Miles the following Mark of
Cattle & Hogs was recorded April 5, 1758
Vizt; a crop on the right ear

Page 108. At the request of Thomas Hilleary the following
Certificate of Stray was recorded April 5, 1758
PGCo Sct, April 3, 1758; Thomas Hilleary brought before me as
a trespasser and stray a small bay mare, bobbed tail, branded
on the near shoulder and buttock. Mordecai Jacob

Page 108. At the request of Zachariah Evans the following Bill
of Sale was recorded April 8, 1758
I Philip Evans, planter in consideration of 15 shillings current
and 3469 pounds crop tobacco paid by Zachariah Evans have
sold 6 cattle, 2 mares and 2 colts, 23 head of hogs, 1 bed and
furniture, 1 large iron pot, 1 pair of hand mill stones, 2 chests.
Signed Philip Evans in the presence of Mary Young, George
Wheeler and acknowledged before Christopher Lowndes

Page 108. At the request of George Cross the following Deed
was recorded April 10, 1758
I John Smith Prather, Gentleman in consideration of 12 current
money paid by George Cross have sold part of a tract called
"Hills Choice" containing 41-1/2 acres and bounded by
"Darnall's Grove." In witness whereof I have set my hand and
seal this March 27, 1758, John Smith Prather in the presence of
and acknowledged before David Ross, Christopher Lowndes
and at the same time Elizabeth Prather wife of John Smith
Prather relinguished her right of dower

Page 110. At the request of John Stone Hawkins the following
Deed was recorded April 11, 1758
Indenture made March 29, 1758; Hezekiah Magruder, planter
in consideration of 80 pounds sterling money of Great Britain
paid by John Stone Hawkins has sold four tracts; the

southernmost fourth part of a tract called "Quick Sale" containing 80 acres; 72 acres lying between "New Exchange" and "Quick Sale" which lands were bequeath to me by my father Alexander Magruder's last will and testament; part of "Anchovies Hills" containing 30 acres and lying near William Mills as by deed from Thomas Swan to me the said Hezekiah Magruder and recorded in Liber EE folio 636-637; and part of "Quick Sale" containing 30 acres and bounded by George Jones land and "Anchovies Hills" as by deed from Thomas Swan to me the said Hezekiah Magruder and recorded in Liber EE folio 636-637. Signed Hezekiah Magruder in the presence of and acknowledged before Mordecai Jacob, Robert Tyler and at the same time Martha Magruder wife of Hezekiah Magruder relinguished her right of dower

Page 111. At the request of William Bowie the following Bill of Sale was recorded April 13, 1758
I Thomas Smith Greenfield, planter in consideration of 23 pounds 6 shillings and 9 pence current money paid by William Bowie have sold Negro lad Nacy (14 yrs.). In witness whereof I have set my hand and seal this March 31, 1758, Thomas Smith Greenfield in the presence of Thomas Williams, Thomas Brooke and acknowledged before Thomas Williams

Page 112. At the request of Margaret Evans the following Deed of Gift was recorded April 19, 1758
I Margaret Evans, widow, for the natural love and affection which I bear my son Seth Evans and for divers other good causes and consideration me hereunto moving have given him a Negro boy called Andrew (8 mo.). But should my son die before he comes to age, then I do give the Negro boy to my son John Grimes, reserving the use and benefit of said Negro during my natural life. In witness whereof I have set my hand and seal this April 13, 1758, Margaret Evans in the presence of and acknowledged before John Hepburn

Page 113. At the request of Henry Lowe the following Bill of Sale was recorded April 19, 1758

I William Windham in consideration of 6 pound 15 shillings current and 200 pounds of tobacco paid by Henry Lowe have sold 2 cows and 2 yearlings and 1 black mare. In witness whereof I have set my hand and seal this April 11, 1758, in the presence of and acknowledged before George Gantt

Page 113. At the request of John Contee the following Deed was recorded April 22, 1758
Indenture made April 20, 1758; Theodore Contee in consideration of 325 pounds sterling money of Great Britain paid by John Contee and in consideration him thereunto moving has sold his part of a tract called "Warburton Manor" containing 425 acres and beginning at a cedar post made on a resurvey June 15, 1725 and binding on Piscattaway Creek at the lower side of Butler's Cove. Signed Theodore Contee, in the presence of and acknowledged before John Cooke, Thomas Williams

Page 115. At the request of Hillery Ball the following Lease was recorded April 22, 1758
Indenture made April 15, 1758; Charles Beall, planter in consideration of the rents and covenants herein hath granted to farm let by these presents to Hillery Ball all that part of two tracts called "Beall's Adventure" and "Barrens" containing 100 acres for 21 years from December 16, 1756 paying yearly on the March 25th the quantity of 700 pounds clean merchantable or inspected tobacco of the lawful gage clear of wood delivered at the warehouse or landing at Bladensburg so long as Hillery Ball and his wife and no other till the premises. Also to plant 100 good apple trees before the expiration of 3 years in a regular enclosed orchard on the south side of ye branch on which ye house stands. Signed Charles Beall, Hillery Ball in the presence of and acknowledged before David Ross, John Cooke

Page 117. At the request of Moses Orme the following Certificate of Stray was recorded April 25, 1758
PGCo Sct, April 24, 1758; This is to certify that Moses Orme brought before me a stray a small chestnut colored horse abt 11 hands high, docked, branded on the near shoulder and buttock,

a large star in his forehead, a ridge main, paces naturally and appears to have one stone left. George Gordon

Page 118.   At the request of Ezekiel Basil the following Certificate of Stray was recorded April 26, 1758
PGCo. Sct; I hereby certify that Ezekiel Basil brought before me a small dark bay mare about 12 hands high, taken up as a stray, neither docked or branded appears to be 4 years old. April 24, 1758

Page 118.   At the request of Thomas Bowman the following Certificate of Stray was recorded May 3, 1758
PGCo Sct; This is to certify that Thomas Bowman brought before me as a stray a bay mare about 10-11 years old branded on the near buttock, a hanging mane and switch tail, about 13 hands high, many saddle spots, both sides gaulded with carrying burthens and has been troublesome to him since November last. April 28, 1758, un-signed

Page 118.   At the request of Thomas King the following Certificate of Stray was recorded May 3, 1758
PGCo Sct, May 3, 1758; I hereby certify that Thomas King near Upper Marlborough Town brought before me a bay horse taken up as a stray about 13 hands high, a star in his forehead, two white feet behind and shod all fours, trots and appears old, crest fallen and no visible brand. Joseph Belt, Jr.

Page 118. At the request of Francis Waring the following Bill of Sale was recorded May 8, 1758
I Thomas Smith Greenfield in consideration of 250 pounds current money paid by Francis Waring, Negroes, Hector, Harry, James, Nacy, Pegg, Isaac and Clement. In witness whereof I have set my hand and seal this May 5, 1758,Thomas Smith Greenfield in the presence of Thomas Contee, George Lee and acknowledged before Thomas Contee

Page 119.   At the request of Benjamin Ray the following Certificate of Stray was recorded May 10, 1758

PGCo Sct, May 6, 1758; Benjamin Ray brought before me a dark bay mare, branded on near buttock, 13 hands high as a trespasser on the plantation of Mrs. Margaret Pile where he is an overseer. John Contee

Page 119. At the request of James Watson the following Deed was recorded May 13, 1758
Indenture made May 10, 1758; Leonard Oliver in consideration of 3 pounds currency paid by James Watson, Sr., planter has sold a tract called "Juxta Stadium Aurectum" containing 50 acres and beginning at the south west corner "Golden Race" it being the being tree. Signed Leonard Oliver in the presence of and acknowledged before George Gantt, Thomas Contee and at the same time Elizabeth Oliver wife of Leonard Oliver relinguished her right of dower

Page 120. At the request of James Marshall the following Bill of Sale was recorded May 13, 1758
I Elizabeth Kelly, widow in consideration of 60 pounds current money paid by James Marshall, merchant has sold two Negroes, Cate (13 yrs.) and Sauk (11 yrs.). In witness whereof I have set my hand and seal this April 28, 1758, Elizabeth Kelly in the presence of George Gordon, Thomas Magruder

Page 120. At the request of Joseph Wallingford the following Certificate of Stray was recorded May 20, 1758
PGCo Sct; I hereby certify that Joseph Wallingford living near Capt. Enoch Magruder, brought before me taken up as a stray a grey mare appears 5-6 years old, under 13 hands high, undocked but branded, also a yearling mare colt that sucks said mare, her color dark grey and not branded. Given under my hand this May 16, 1758, John Cooke

Page 121. At the request of Abraham Clark the following Certificate of Stray was recorded May 13, 1758
PGCo Sct, May 9, 1758; Abraham Clark, Jr., brought before me a small sorrel horse as a trespasser and stray, branded on the near shoulder, a small star in his forehead and a white speck on

his near thigh. Mordecai Jacob

Page 121. At the request of Jeremiah Magruder the following Deed was recorded May 27, 1758
Indenture made May 23, 1758; David Weems of Anne Arundel County, Maryland, Gentleman in consideration of 146 pounds 6 shillings and 6 pence sterling Great Britain paid by Jeremiah Magruder has sold part of a tract called "Porke Hall" formerly lying in Calvert County, Maryland and now in PGCo containing 162-3/4 acres and beginning at a bounded tree of "Porke Hall," "Beall's Reserve" (now in possession of Thomas Moore) "Brazon Thorpe Hall" (now in possession of Thomas Harwood) and the second bound tree of "Brough." Signed David Weems, in the presence of John Hepburn, Lock Weems and acknowledged before John Hepburn and at the same time Easter Weems wife of David Weems relinguished her right of dower

Page 123. At the request of John Grindall the following Deed was recorded May 17, 1758
Indenture made May 10, 1758; Samuel Roundell, merchant in consideration of 6000 pounds of tobacco paid by John Grindall has sold part of a tract called "Taylors Coast" containing 111 acres and lying between the north branch of Swanson's Creek and Aquasco Manor and beginning at land surveyed for George Lingan, Esqr., deceased and bounded by "Poplar Hills." Signed Samuel Roundell, in the presence of and acknowledged before George Gantt, Thomas Contee and at the same time Martha Roundell wife of Samuel Roundell relinguished her right of dower

Page 124. At the request of Charles Willett the following Certificate of Stray was recorded May 17, 1758
PGCo Sct; I hereby certify that Charles Willett brought before me a bay horse, 13 hands high, a star in his forehead, a snip, branded on the oft buttock. May 23, 1758, Robert Tyler

Page 124. At the request of John Mayhew the following Certificate of Stray was recorded May 27, 1758

PGCo Sct; John Mayhew, near Upper Marlborough Town brought before me a small black horse take up as a stray, 8-10 years old, a large star and two white feet behind, branded on the near buttock. May 23, 1758, Joseph Belt, Jr.

Page 124. At the request of William Brown the following Certificate of Stray was recorded May 28, 1758
March 28, 1758; William Brown brought before me a dark bay horse about 12-1/2 hands high, a small blaze in his face, not docked or branded, is troublesome and breaks into his inclosures. Christopher Lowndes

Page 124. At the request of Thomas Gordon the following Certificate of Stray was recorded June 10, 1758
PGCo Sct; I hereby certify that Mr. Thomas Gordon brought before me as a stray a small dark brown colored horse, branded on his near shoulder, 5 years old, does not pace. June 7, 1758, John Cooke

Page 124. At the request of John Riddle, Jr. the following Certificate of Stray was recorded June 12, 1758
PGCo Sct, June 9, 1858; John Riddle, Jr. brought before me a middle sized bay horse as a trespasser and stray branded on the near buttock and shoulder, several saddle spots, and appears old. Mordecai Jacob

Page 124. At the request of Ignatius Ransom the following Deed was recorded June 12, 1758
Indenture made May 18, 1758; George Naylor, planter in consideration of 7000 pounds of inspected crop tobacco paid by Ignatius Ransom, planter has sold part of two tracts, "Forrest of Fancy" and "Juxta Stadium Aurectum" containing 92 acres and lying on the west side of Patuxent River. Signed George Naylor in the presence of John Hepburn, Samuel Chew Hepburn and acknowledged before John Hepburn and at the same time Lettice Naylor wife of George Naylor relinguished her right of dower

Page 126a. At the request of George Naylor the following Deed was recorded June 14, 1758
Indenture made May 13, 1758, James Watson, planter, in consideration of 7000 pounds of inspected crop tobacco paid by George Naylor has sold part of two tracts, "Forrest of Fancy" and "Juxta Stadium Aurectum" containing 92 acres and lying on the west side of Patuxent River. Signed James Watson in the presence of John Hepburn, Moses Orme and acknowledged before John Hepburn

Page 126b. At the request of James Buckman the following Certificate of Stray was recorded June 16, 1758
PGCo Sct, June 16, 1758; James Buckman brought before me a dark bay or blackish horse, 13 hands high, branded on the off buttock, one white foot behind and a small star in his forehead and complains he is troublesome and breaks into his inclosures. Christopher Lowndes

Page 126b. At the request of Luke Church the following Deed of Gift was recorded June 16, 1758
I William Ellis, schoolmaster for divers good causes me hereunto moving have given by these presents unto Mary Church wife of Luke Church, planter, 1 black mare. In witness whereof I have set my hand and seal this May 8, 1758, William Ellis in the presence of Gerard T. Greenfield

Page 126b. At the request of George Bowdon, Attorney for Edward Trafford, Esqr. & Sons the following Bill of Sale was recorded June 17, 1758
I John Sutton, Gentleman in consideration of 15,940 light pounds crop tobacco paid by Edward Trafford, Esqr. & Sons of Liverpool, merchants, have sold Negroes and premises as follows; Beck (35 yrs.), Jeffry (12 yrs.), Cheshire (10 yrs.) and Ben (7 yrs.), 2 bed stocks, 2 feather beds with blankets, sheets, quilts and rugs, 1 walnut desk and 1 black mare. In witness whereof I have set my hand and seal this June 7, 1758, John Sutton in the presence of and acknowledged before George Gordon, George Hardey, Jr.

Acknowledged by George Bowdon, Attorney in fact for Edward Trafford, Esqr. & Sons of Liverpool,

Page 127. At the request of George Naylor the following Land Commission was recorded abt June 17, 1758
Memorandum that on the special petition of George Naylor preferred to the justices of Prince George's County, Maryland on the 4th Tuesday in June in the 7th year of his Lordship commission the Right Hon. the Lord Proprietary Dominion etc., his Lordship commission issued by order of the justices aforesaid out of the county aforesaid on the 7th day of July Anno Domini 1757. In these words following, Frederick Absolute Lord and Proprietary of the Province of Maryland and Avalon Lord Baron of Baltimore vizt; to Messrs Thomas Contee, William Eversfield, William Deakins and Richard Estep of PGCo Gentleman, whereas George Naylor, is seized of a tract called "Smith's Pasture" and preferred his petition in writing to our county court held at Upper Marlborough Town before Peter Dent, Gentleman and his associates then and still justices within our county to examine evidence to prove and perpetuate the memory of the bounds of the said tract of land. Therefore, we command you any three or two of you to examine all witnesses or persons concerned touching their knowledge of the bounds of the said tract. Witness John Contee, Gentleman, June 30, 1757. Issued July 7, 1757, Joseph Sim, Clk
Advertisement, by virtue of a commission to examine evidences to prove the bounds of "Smith's Pasture" we hereby give notice that we intend to meet at the lands on Monday, September 5th next. Witness our hands and seals this August 6, 1757, William Eversfield, William Deakins, Richard Estep
Thomas Lawson aged 69 years or thereabouts declares that about 14 years ago, Thomas Wall, deceased told him that a large live oak standing on the south west side of Wall's plantation within 20 yards of the main road that leads to Piscattaway was a bounded tree of his land and further saith not. Thomas Lawson, William Eversfield, Richard Estep, William Deakins
Robert Wall, aged 59 or thereabouts says that about 10 years ago his father Thomas Wall, deceased told him that a large live

oak standing on the south west side of Wall's plantation within 20 yards of the main road that leads to Piscattaway was a bounded tree of his land and further saith not. Thomas Lawson, William Eversfield, William Deakins, Richard Estep

Mary Wall aged 70 years or thereabouts declares about 10 years ago her husband Thomas Wall, deceased told her that a large live oak standing on the south west side of Wall's plantation within 20 yards of the main road that leads to Piscattaway was a bounded tree of his land and further saith not. Thomas Lawson, William Eversfield, William Deakins, Richard Estep

Page 129. At the request of Luke Mudd the following Supersedes was recorded June 27, 1758
You Luke Mudd and Thomas Sansberry, Jr., do confess judgment to Benjamin Early for the sum of 400 pounds of tobacco and 9-1/2 bushels of Indian corn which sum was recovered on June 23, 1757 before me one of His Lordships Justices of the Peace to be levied on your goods chattels lands or tenements for the use of Benjamin Early in case Luke Mudd shall not pay and satisfy the said sum and costs thereon on February 10th next. George Gordon

Page 129. At the request of Thomas Welsh the following Supersedes was recorded June 28, 1758
You Thomas Welsh, William Hall and William Tannehill do confess judgment to Frederick Lord Baltimore for the sum of 16 pound 8 shillings and 10 pence 3 farthing sterling and 1 shilling current money and 364-1/4 pounds of tobacco which sums were recovered on ye fourth Tuesday of March last to be levied on your goods chattels lands or tenements for the use of Frederick Lord Baltimore in case Thomas Welsh shall not pay and satisfy the said sum and costs thereon on February 10th next. John Cooke, Christopher Lowndes

Page 130. At the request of John Brightwell the following Deed was recorded June 28, 1758
Indenture made June 28, 1758; Between Thomas Baden

(Attorney in fact for Sacheverell Wood of the City of Philadelphia, Pennsylvania) and John Brightwell of PGCo. Whereas Sacheverell Wood of the City of Philadelphia, Pennsylvania has appointed Thomas Baden has attorney to deliver and acknowledge a deed of all his right to a tract called "Wood's Farm" lying near Nottingham to John Brightwell, said Power of Attorney recorded in Liber F folio 449. Now this indenture witnesseth that Thomas Baden, in consideration of 150 pounds current money paid by John Brightwell has sold all that parcel of land called "Wood's Farm" containing 345 acres. Signed Thomas Baden, Attorney in fact for Sacheverell Wood in the presence of and acknowledged before John Baden

Record of Pennsylvania Marriages Prior to 1810, Volume 2, By John B. Linn, William H. Egle
Christ Church, Philadelphia, Pennsylvania
Sacheverell Wood m. Mary Hawkins December 11, 1759

Page 131. At the request of Richard Edelen & Christopher Edelen the following Bond was recorded June 28, 1758;
I William Hicks of St. Mary's County, Maryland, merchant and held and firmly bound unto Richard Edelen and Christopher Edelen the one of Charles County, Maryland and the other of PGCo, planters in the full and just sum of 38,000 pounds of tobacco and 100 pounds sterling money for the payment to which to be well and truly done and made thereby bind myself by these presents, sealed and dated this December 2, 1757.
The condition of the above is that whereas William Hicks hath agreed with Richard Edelen & Christopher Edelen for 300 acres of land to Richard Edelen and for 312-1/2 acres of land with Christopher Edelen being three fourths of the quantity of land they held in a parcel called "Calvert's Manor" lying in PGCo. If the bounded William Hicks do and shall when required well and truly convey to the said Richard Edelen & Christopher Edelen the aforesaid land by a sufficient deed of general warranty then the above obligation to be void. Signed William Hicks in the presence of Richard B. Boarman, James Edelen

Page 131. At the request of Richard Edelen the following Deed was recorded June 28, 1758

Indenture made June 8, 1758; between William Hicks of St. Mary's County, Maryland, merchant of one part and Richard Edelen of Charles County, Maryland, planter of the other part. Witnesseth whereas William Hicks hath by virtue of the award of Messrs Thomas Marshall, Bayne Smallwood and John Stoddert of Charles County, Maryland, Gentlemen, arbitrators indifferently elected and named between the said William Hicks and the parties possessed of 2,400 acres of land part of a tract of 3,000 acres formerly granted to William Calvert Esqr., commonly called "Piscattaway Manor" otherwise "Calvert's Manor," alias "Elizabeth Manor," recovered 1800 acres. Whereas the named Richard Edelen was in possession of a part of the manor formerly belonging to Edward Edelen on the second line (or back line) and bounded on the 600 acres of land in possession of Thomas Noble and George Noble and containing 203 acres. And whereas Richard Edelen hath agreed to purchase of William Hicks the 3/4ths of the same awarded to William Hicks. This indenture therefore further witnesseth that William Hicks in consideration of 45 pounds 13 shillings and 6 pence sterling money by Richard Edelen has sold the aforesaid 203 acres. And lastly William Hicks will warrant the 153 acres of the aforesaid parcel.

Signed William Hicks in the presence of Robert Hammett, Basil Biscoe and acknowledged before Robert Hammett, James Biscoe, JP's of St. Mary's County, Maryland and at the same time Priscilla Hicks wife of William Hicks relinquished her right of dower

Page 133. At the request of Thomas Marshall the following Deed was recorded June 29, 1758

Indenture made June 8, 1758; William Hicks of St. Mary's County, Maryland, merchant in consideration of 34 pounds 12 shillings and six pence sterling by Thomas Marshall has sold part of a tract taken up by William Calvert, Esq. lying on Piscattaway Creek known by the name of Calvert's Manor containing 170 acres being that part now in the possession of

James Edelen which said parcel of land William Hicks came to in fee simple. Signed William Hicks in the presence of Robert Hammett, Basil Biscoe and acknowledged before Robert Hammett, James Biscoe, JP's of St. Mary's County, Maryland and at the same time Priscilla Hicks wife of William Hicks relinquished her right of dower

Page 135. At the request of Christopher Edelen the following Deed was recorded June 29, 1758
Indenture made June 8, 1758; between William Hicks of St. Mary's County, Maryland, merchant of one part and Christopher Edelen of PGCo, planter of the other part. Witnesseth whereas William Hicks hath by virtue of the award of Messrs Thomas Marshall, Bayne Smallwood and John Stoddert of Charles County, Maryland, Gentlemen, arbitrators indifferently elected and named between the said William Hicks and the parties possessed of 2,400 acres of land part of a tract of 3,000 acres formerly granted to William Calvert Esqr., commonly called "Piscattaway Manor" otherwise "Calvert's Manor," alias "Elizabeth Manor," recovered 1800 acres. Whereas the named Christopher Edelen was in possession of a part of the manor beginning at the end of the first course of Richard Edelen's on the second line (or back line) and bounded on the 600 acres of land in possession of Thomas Noble and George Noble and containing 176 acres. And whereas Christopher Edelen hath agreed to purchase of William Hicks the 3/4ths of the same awarded to William Hicks. This indenture therefore further witnesseth that William Hicks in consideration of 34 pounds 12 shillings and 6 pence sterling money by Christopher Edelen has sold the aforesaid 176 acres. And lastly, William Hicks will warrant the 138-1/2 acres Signed William Hicks in the presence of Robert Hammett, Basil Biscoe and acknowledged before Robert Hammett, James Biscoe, JP's of St. Mary's County, Maryland and at the same time Priscilla Hicks wife of William Hicks relinquished her right of dower

Page 137. At the request of George Maxwell the following Deed was recorded June 29, 1758

Indenture made June 28, 1758; John Lang, planter of PGCo in consideration of 50 pounds sterling paid by George Maxwell, merchant of Charles County, Maryland has sold a parcel of land formerly lying in Calvert County, Maryland and now in PGCo called "Popleton" containing 200 acres and lying on the west side of Patuxent River. Signed John Lang in the presence of and acknowledged before John Cooke, George Gordon

Page 138. At the request of John Emerson the following Deed was recorded June 29, 1758
Indenture made June 13, 1758; Charles Fenley, planter in consideration of 24 pounds sterling money of Great Britain paid by John Emerson, planter has sold a tract called "Nonesuch" containing 136 acres and lying on a ridge between Piscattaway Creek and Mattawoman Swamp on both sides of the roads that leads from the head of Piscattaway Creek to Pomonkey. Signed Charles Fenley in the presence of James Marshall, George Gantt and acknowledged before George Gantt, George Gordon

Page 139. At the request of John Bullman the following Supersedes was recorded June 28, 1758
You John Bullman, John McGill and John Carrick do confess judgment to Zachariah Lyles for the sum of 427 pounds of tobacco debt and 2/6 cost which sums were recovered on the 24th day of this instant before me one of His Lordships Justices of the Peace to be levied on your goods chattels lands or tenements for the use of Zachariah Lyles in case John Bullman shall not pay and satisfy the said sum and costs thereon on February 10th next. Taken and acknowledged this May 30th 1758, Mordecai Jacob

Page 140. At the request of John Lucksin the following Deed was recorded June 28, 1758
Indenture made June 28, 1758; Philip Evans, planter in consideration of 22 pounds one shilling and seven pence current money paid by John Lucksin, planter has sold a tract called "Proventiall" containing 92 acres and beginning on the east line of "Littleworth." Signed Philip Evans, Sr., in the

presence of and acknowledged before Nathaniel Magruder, George Gantt and at the same time {un-named} wife of Philip Evans relinquished her right of dower

Page 141. At the request of James Marshall the following Deed was recorded June 29, 1758
Indenture made June 13, 1758; John Moore and Sarah Moore his wife in consideration of 210 pounds sterling money of Great Britain paid by James Marshall has sold two tracts, part of "The Strife" which was by deed of division between Thomas Addison and Gabriel Parker and Ann Parker his wife of Calvert County, Maryland, recorded in 1725 and part of "Partnership" being that portion which Ann Parker of Calvert County, Maryland, widow gave to her daughter Sarah Parker. Signed John Moore, Sarah Moore in the presence of and acknowledged before George Gordon, George Gantt and at the same time Sarah Moore wife of John Moore relinquished her right of dower

Page 142. At the request of Barton Lucas the following Bill of Sale was recorded June 29, 1758
We Henrietta Queen and Henry Queen, executors of Samuel Queen, late of PGCo, deceased in consideration that this day paid acquitted and discharged the sundry debts which said Samuel Queen became bound on the accounts of said Barton Lucas to Mr. Robert Peter. To secure and indemnify the Samuel Queen for the debt, the said Barton conveyed to Samuel Queen four Negroes, Jean, George, Amy and Simon. Also hog, cattle, household furniture as by a Bill of Sale will more fully appear. Now know ye that we the said executors in consideration of the several sums of money and tobacco being paid have re-conveyed the above Negroes, hog, cattle, household furniture to Barton Lucas. In witness whereof I have set my hand and seal this June 9, 1758, Henrietta Queen, Henry Queen, in the presence of Sarah Jenkins, William Queen

Page 142. At the request of James Crafford the following Deed was recorded June 29, 1758
Indenture made June 8, 1758; William Beanes of PGCo in

77

consideration of 27,580 pounds of tobacco paid by James Crafford of Frederick County, Maryland has sold part of a tract called "Grove Hurst" containing 394 acres lying on the south side of a branch near John Norton's and bounded by the northeast corner tree of "Lordships Manor." Signed William Beanes in the presence of John Hepburn, Benjamin Berry, Jr., and acknowledged before John Hepburn and at the same time Elizabeth Beanes wife of William Beanes relinquished her right of dower

Page 144. At the request of James Burnes the following Bill of Sale was recorded June 30, 1758
I Barton Lucas in consideration of 80 pounds current money of Maryland and 10,202 pounds of tobacco paid by James Burnes have sold three Negroes, Jean, George and Amy. Also 30 hogs, three cows and calves, one bed and furniture, three iron pots and two draught horses. In witness whereof I have hereunto set my hand and seal this June 10, 1758, Barton Lucas in the presence of John Flint, Thomas Flint

Page 144. At the request of Joseph Belt, 3rd the following Certificate of Stray was recorded June 30, 1758
I certify that Joseph Belt, 3rd, brought before me a small black horse as a trespasser and stray, branded on the near thigh has a small white spot on his off thigh. June 26, 1758, Thomas Williams

Page 144. At the request of Reverend John Eversfield the following Deed was recorded July 1, 1758
I John Eversfield, Rector of St. Paul's Parish in consideration of the natural love and paternal affection which I bear unto my son William Eversfield, an infant as also for in consideration of five shillings current money of Maryland by his brother-in-law William Eversfield has given unto my son William Eversfield, an infant, the following tracts and parts of several tracts of lands adjoining to each other, vizt; a tract of land purchased of Gerard Truman Greenfield called "Golden Race" containing 179 acres as by deed bearing date November 26, 1753; also three tracts of

land, one called "The Forrest" purchased by Messrs. Thomas Swann, Sr., and Thomas Swann, Jr. containing 197 acres, the second called "The Bite" containing 25 acres as by deed bearing date September 26, 1754; the third called "Eversfield's Swamp" taken up by myself and duly patented and abutting on the two former tracts containing 10-1/2 acres as by certificate of survey bearing date March 31, 1757; also three parts of a tract called "Gedling", part of a tract called "Whims Acre" and part of a tract called "Archers Pasture" purchased of Mr. George Parker containing 324 acres by deed bearing date March 11, 1754. In witness whereof I have hereunto set my hand and seal this July 1, 1750; John Eversfield in the presence of John Hepburn, Thomas Blacklock and acknowledged before John Hepburn

Page 146. At the request of Reverend John Eversfield the following Deed was recorded July 1, 1758 Indenture made July 1, 1758;I Thomas Blacklock, planter in consideration of 2000 pounds of good merchantable tobacco in half crop and the other half crop transfer paid by Rev. John Eversfield, clerk has sold part of a tract called "Blacklock's Venture" containing 33 acres and bounded by "Widows Trouble." Signed Thomas Blacklock in the presence of John Hepburn, John England and acknowledged before John Hepburn and at the same time Charity Blacklock wife of Thomas Blacklock relinquished her right of dower

Page 147. At the request of Deborah Eversfield the following Deed was recorded July 5, 1758
I John Eversfield, Rector of St. Paul's parish in consideration of the natural love and paternal affection which I bear unto my daughter Deborah Eversfield and for diverse other good causes and considerations me thereunto moving has given three parts of two tracts, vizt; Widows Trouble the plantation whereon Thomas Hagan lately dwelt and purchased of said Hagan and Margaret Hagan his wife by deed bearing date February 14, 1757 containing 196 acres; also to parts of two tracts formerly called "Poormans Industry" and "Casteel" but now by a resurvey lately made by Edmund Casteel united into one entire tract

79

called by the name of "Edmonds Frolick" containing 101 acres; and another part of "Edmonds Frolick" containing 26 acres purchased of Edmund Casteel by two deeds bearing date June 8, 1757. To have and to hold and for default of heirs to Matthew Eversfield and for default of heirs to Charles Eversfield and for default of heirs to William Eversfield and for default of heirs to the Rev. John Eversfield, Jr. and for default of heirs to me the donor excepting my wife Eleanor Eversfield as to her right of dower in case of survivorship. In witness whereof I have hereunto set my hand and seal this July 1, 1758, John Eversfield in the presence of John Hepburn, Thomas Blacklock and acknowledged before John Hepburn

Page 149.   At the request of Reverend John Eversfield the following Deed was recorded July 5, 1758
I John Eversfield, rector of St. Paul's Parish in consideration of the natural love and paternal affection which I bear unto my son Matthew Eversfield also in consideration of five shillings currency by William Eversfield his brother-in-law in his behalf does give the following tract and parts of several tracts lying contiguous and adjoining each other vizt; a tract purchased of Richard Wright and Jane Wright his wife called "The Farm" containing 50 acres by deed bearing date July 18, 1753. Also three parts of several tracts, to wit, "Gedling," "Gedling and Archers Pasture" and containing 177 acres by deed bearing date October 13, 1757; with two parts of two tracts called "Quick Sale" and "Archers Pasture" adjacent to each other and purchased of Richard Kirkwood and containing 150 acres by deed bearing date February 2, 1757; lastly one part of a tract called "Quick Sale" purchased of Peregrine Mackaness and containing 90-1/2 acres by deed bearing date October 11, 1751. To have and to hold the aforesaid tracts and for default of heirs to William Eversfield an infant and for default of heirs to Charles Eversfield and for default of heirs to Rev. John Eversfield, Jr. and for default of such heirs to me the donor excepting my wife Eleanor Eversfield as to her right of dower in case of survivorship. In witness whereof I have hereunto set my hand and seal this July 1, 1758, John Eversfield in the presence of John

Hepburn, Thomas Blacklock and acknowledged before John Hepburn

Page 151. At the request of Thomas Marshall the following Mortgage was recorded July 30, 1758
Indenture made July 3, 1758; Leonard Marbury, planter of PGCo in consideration of 53 pounds five shillings sterling money of Great Britain paid by Thomas Marshall of Charles County, Maryland has sold four Negroes; Sue, Ben, Henriettor (5 yrs.), and Nacy (1 yr.), provided that Leonard Marbury shall well and truly pay unto Thomas Marshall the aforesaid sum of money at or before June 22, 1759 then this indenture to be void. Signed Leonard Marbury in the presence of George Gantt, William Mallow and acknowledged before George Gantt

Page 151. At the request of Thomas Cramphin the following Deed was recorded July 15, 1758
Indenture made July 4, 1758; Elizabeth Batt, Gentlewoman in consideration of 25 pounds sterling money of Great Britain paid by Thomas Cramphin has sold a tract called "Elizabeth's Delight" being a lot of Notley Rozer, Esqr., 1000 acres of land set up in his 2000 pound lottery divided into 8 lots distinguished in the scheme of the lottery by the letter "G" and containing 100 acres. Signed Elizabeth Batt in the presence of and acknowledged before George Gantt, Thomas Contee

Page 153. At the request of Isaac Lansdale the following Mortgage was recorded July 15, 1758
I Jeremiah Crabb, planter in consideration of 110 pounds sterling paid by Isaac Lansdale, Gentleman do bargain and sell and deliver Mulatto Clement, Rachel, Jacob and Negroes Cesar, Kate and Cloe provided nevertheless that if Jeremiah Crabb shall well and truly pay unto Isaac Lansdale the aforesaid sum of money before the first day of March next then this present Bill of Sale to be void. In witness whereof I have hereunto set my hand and seal this July 11, 1758, Jeremiah Crabb, in the presence of Mordecai Jacob, James Drane and acknowledged before Mordecai Jacob

Page 153. At the request of James Marshall the following Deed was recorded July 16, 1758
Indenture made June 29, 1758; between John Abington, planter and James Marshall, merchant. Witnessed that whereas John Abington did stand indebted unto several persons and sundry sums of money amounting in the whole to 296 pounds current money of Maryland which James Marshall at the special instance and request of the said John Abington had paid and satisfied and discharged in consideration thereof and also the sum of five shillings current money has sold unto James Marshall three tracts of land, to wit, "Goodwill" containing 190 acres, "Speedwell" containing 138 acres and "Irvine" containing 150 acres. Provided nevertheless that if John Abington shall well and truly pay unto James Marshall the said sum of money with legal interest on or before June 1, 1759 this deed shall being null and void. Signed John Abington in the presence of John Hepburn, John Watson and acknowledged before John Hepburn and at the same time Nancy Abington wife of John Abington relinquished her right of dower

Page 155. At the request of Isaac Lansdale the following Deed was recorded July 15, 1758
Indenture made May 3, 1758; between Priscilla Crabb, widow late the wife of Ralph Crabb Gentleman deceased and Edward Crabb one of the sons of Ralph Crabb of the one part and Isaac Lansdale, planter of the other part. Witnessed that whereas Priscilla Crabb stands seized for the term of her natural life tracts called "James Lot" and "Williams Lot" being part of "Essington" by the last will and testament of Ralph Crabb and after her death to revert to Edward Crabb. Now the said Priscilla Crabb and Edward Crabb in consideration of 71 pounds 16 shillings sterling and 8 pounds five shillings and six pence three farthing's currency paid by Isaac Lansdale has sold "James Lot" containing 156 acres being part of "Essington" and beginning on the west side of the rolling road near where John Boyd's road stands and bounded by John Boyd's School House, the lower end of "Cattail Meadows" it being the northwest corner of a tract formerly belonging to Abraham Clark called "Essington." Also

"Williams Lot" containing 40 acres being part of "Essington" beginning near Fanners old field, bounded by "James Lot" and the rolling road from the head of the river. Provided nevertheless it Priscilla Crabb and Edward Crabb shall well and truly pay unto Isaac Lansdale the aforesaid sum of money then this indenture to be void and of non-effect. Signed Priscilla Crabb, Edward Crabb in the presence of and acknowledged before Mordecai Jacob, Robert Tyler

Page 158. At the request of Edward Osborn the following Certificate of Stray was recorded July 27, 1758
PGCo Sct, July 24, 1758; I hereby certify Edward Osborn brought before me a small dark bay mare about 12-1/2 hands high, branded on the near buttock and shoulder, has her right eye put out and taken up as a stray. Robert Tyler

Page 158. At the request of Richard Henderson the following Deed was recorded July 29, 1758
I John Halsall in consideration of 2500 pounds crop tobacco paid by Richard Henderson factor for John Glassford & Company have sold Negro boy Jem (10 yrs.). In witness whereof I have hereunto set my hand and affixed my seal this July 14, 1758, John Halsall in the presence of Josias Beall, Margaret Carnes and acknowledged before Christopher Lowndes

Page 159. At the request of William Mockbee the following Certificate of Stray was recorded July 29, 1758
PGCo Sct, July 29, 1758; William Mockbee brought before me a dark colored mare about 12 hands high, branded on the off thigh which he found trespassing. Nathaniel Magruder

Page 159. At the request of Eleanor Piles the following Marks of her Creatures was recorded July 29, 1758
A crop and hole and under and over bit in the left ear and an under bit in the right ear

Page 159. At the request of John Watson the following Certificate of Stray was recorded July 29, 1758

83

PGCo Sct, July 25, 1758; Mr. John Watson brought before me a chestnut sorrel horse about 12 hands high, branded aged about 10 years he complains he is troublesome and breaks into his enclosures. He had on a large old bell and a country made iron buckle. Christopher Lowndes

Page 159. At the request of John Tucker the following Certificate of Stray was recorded July 31, 1758
PGCo Sct, July 31, 1758; I hereby certify that John Tucker brought before me as a stray a small iron gray mare who says she has trespassed upon him for two years, is now on broke and appears to be five or six years old, docked and branded on the off buttock. John Cooke

Page 159. At the request of Lancelot Willson the following Certificate of Stray was recorded August 5, 1758
PGCo Sct, August 2, 1758; Lancelot Willson complains that a stray cow with a white star in her forehead uses his plantation and is troublesome. She is about eight or nine years old. Christopher Lowndes

Page 159. At the request of Thomas Wilson the following Deed of Gift was recorded August 7, 1758
I Elizabeth Dryden and consideration of the love goodwill and affection which I do bear towards my loving son in law Thomas Wilson has given and assigns all my household and chattels with all my other creatures to him. In witness whereof I have hereunto set my hand and seal this March 1, 1758, Elizabeth Dryden
Test: John Wiglitt, W. Brown

Page 160. At the request of George Maxwell the following Deed was recorded August 12, 1758
Indenture made August 12, 1758; Richard Hutton, tailor of PGCo in consideration of 3500 pounds of crop tobacco paid by George Maxwell, merchant of Charles County, Maryland has sold part of a tract called "Hatchett" which John Willson formerly sold and conveyed to John Haggarty containing 76

84

acres and beginning near the road side that leads into the neck where Capt. Samuel Perrie's dwelling house formerly stood and in the line and that divides the said "Hatchett" with a tract of land formerly belonging to Samuel Waring and thence to a line of a tract formerly belonging to Bernard Johnson. Signed Richard Hutton in the presence of John Hepburn, Benjamin Berry and acknowledged before John Hepburn and at the same time Margaret Hutton wife of Richard Hutton relinquished her right of dower

Page 161. At the request of William Piles the following Bond was recorded August 14, 1758
We Richard Piles and Francis Piles, 3rd, planters are firmly bound unto William Piles, planter in the full and just sum of 30 pounds current money of Maryland this July 15, 1758. The condition of the above obligation is such that whereas William Piles having leased unto his brothers the aforesaid Richard Piles and Francis Piles two tracts for the term therein mentioned. Now know ye that if Richard Piles and Francis Piles do no way molest or disturb the said William Piles in the remaining part of the land then the present obligation to be null void and non-effect. Signed Richard Piles, Francis Piles in the presence of John Hepburn, Isaac Lansdale

Page 162. At the request of Joseph Sprigg & Rachel Sprigg the following Deed was recorded August 22, 1758
Indenture made August 9, 1758; between Clement Hill, Gentleman of the first part, Joseph Sprigg of Gentleman of the second part and Rachel Sprigg, widow of the third part. Witnessed that Clement Hill in consideration of 10 pounds sterling paid by Joseph Sprigg has released and forever one moiety or half part of a parcel of land being part of a tract called "Spy Park Enlarged" lying on the Western branch of Patuxent River and the other moiety or half part to the said Rachel Sprigg during her natural life and to any child of her body she shall give it at her decease containing 8 acres with the water mill. Signed Clement Hill, Joseph Sprigg, Rachel Sprigg in the presence of John Hepburn, Joseph Belt, Jr., and acknowledged before John

Page 163. At the request of Charles Carroll, Jr. the following Deed was recorded August 22, 1758
Indenture made August 16, 1758; Anne Young, widow in consideration of five shillings sterling paid by Charles Carroll has sold all that tract called "Cerne Abbey Manor" containing 1800 acres and of which land a recovery was had at Annapolis in April term last in which Henry Darnall, Esq. was demanded against John Darnall, Esq. who vouch to warranty Anne Young the party to these presents which said tract was heretofore on the February 12, 1663 granted unto George Thompson in three several tracts or divisions of lands the one called "Duddington Manor" said to contain 1000 acres, another called "New Troy" said to contain 500 acres and the third called "Duddington Pasture" containing 300 acres and on May 1, 1671, Gentleman joined and consolidated the three tracts together by the name of "Cerne Abbey Manor." Signed Anne Youngin the presence of John Hepburn, Ignatius Digges and acknowledged before John Hepburn

Page 163. At the request of Edward Trafford, Esqr. & Sons the following Bill of Sale was recorded August 23, 1758
I Ann Downing, widow in consideration of 5543 pounds of crop tobacco paid by Edward Trafford, Esq., & Sons of Liverpool have sold Negro man Sharper. In witness whereof I have set my hand and seal this August 12, 1758, Ann Downing in the presence of Mary Lawrence, George Hardy, Jr.

Page 164. At the request of John Brashear, Sr. the following Supersedes was recorded August 23, 1758
You John Brashear, Sr., John Wells and Paul Rankin and do confess judgment to John Gibson for the sum of seven pound 10 shillings currency debt and 199 ¾ of a pound of tobacco and six pence currency cost which sums were recovered on the fourth Tuesday in June last to be levied on your goods chattels lands or tenements for the use of John Gibson in case John Brashear, Sr. shall not pay and satisfy the said sum and costs thereon on

February 10th next. Mordecai Jacob, Robert Tyler

Page 164. At the request of John Brashear, Sr. the following Supersedes was recorded August 23, 1758
You John Brashear, Sr., William Ducker and Paul Rankin do confess judgment to James Beck, Jr. for the sum of 1 pound 15 shillings and 6 pence currency which sum was recovered before me one of His Lordships Justices of the Peace to be levied on your goods chattels lands or tenements for the use of James Beck, Jr. in case John Brashear, Sr. shall not pay and satisfy the said sum and costs thereon on February 10th next. Robert Tyler

Page 164. At the request of Benjamin Brashear the following Supersedes was recorded August 23, 1758
You Benjamin Brashear, Jeremiah Crabb and John Brashear, Sr., do confess judgment to James Dick, James Mouat and James Nicholson for the sum of six pounds 15 shillings and 6 pence currency debt and 204 ½ pounds of tobacco and six pence currency cost which sums were recovered on the fourth Tuesday in June last to be levied on your goods chattels lands or tenements for the use of James Dick, James Mouat and James Nicholson in case Benjamin Brashear shall not pay and satisfy the said sum and costs thereon on February 10th next. Mordecai Jacob, Robert Tyler

Page 165. At the request of William Murdock the following Certificate of Stray was recorded August 24, 1758
PGCo Sct, August 24, 1758; I hereby certify William Murdock, Esqr., brought before me a small white horse taken up as a stray, branded on the near buttock, has one eye and appears to be old. August 23, 1758, Joseph Belt, Jr.

Page 165. At the request of Shadrack Lanham the following Certificate of Stray was recorded August 24, 1758
PGCo Sct, August 24, 1758; Shadrack Lanham brought before me a stray sorrel mare about 12 hands high, branded on the near buttock has an old white snip on her nose and four white feet, he complains she is troublesome and breaks into his

87

enclosures. Christopher Lowndes

Page 165. At the request of John Mockbee the following Certificate of Stray was recorded August 23, 1758
PGCo Sct, August 23, 1758; I hereby certify that John Mockbee brought before me a small stray white mare seems near blind in one eye, branded. August 22, 1758, J. Sprigg

Page 165. At the request of Jeremiah Crabb the following Deed was recorded August 23, 1758
Indenture made August 7, 1758; John Brashear of Anne Arundel County, Maryland, planter and Thomas Brashear of PGCo, planter in consideration of 6 pounds five shillings current money of Maryland paid by Jeremiah Crabb has sold 1/4 acre, being part of Lot Number 36, lying in Prince George's County in Queen Anne Town on Patuxent River and sold by Robert Tyler. Signed John Brashear, Thomas Brashear, Jr. in the presence of John Hepburn, Thomas Somes and acknowledged before John Hepburn.
August 17, 1758, then came Mary Brashear wife of John Brashear and Mary Brashear wife of Thomas Brashear relinquished her right of dower. Mordecai Jacob, Robert Tyler

Page 166. At the request of Anne Young the following Lease was recorded August 23, 1758
Indenture made August 17, 1758; Charles Carroll, Jr., in consideration of five shillings sterling paid by Anne Young, widow has sold part of a tract called "Cerne Abbey Manor" called "Duddington Manor," "New Troy" and "Duddington Pasture" or whatever name containing 400 acres and where her dwelling house now stands. Beginning at the fork of St. James Creek and running along the river to Turkey Buzzard Point. To have and to hold from this date for and during the term of 1 year paying 1 pepper corn yearly at the feast of St. Michael the Arch Angel. Signed Charles Carrol, Jr., in the presence of John Hepburn, William Elson and acknowledged before John Hepburn

Page 167. At the request of Anne Young the following Release was recorded August 23, 1758
Indenture made August 18, 1758; Charles Carroll, Jr., Esqr., in consideration of 10 shillings paid by Anne Young, widow has released in her actual possession by virtue of a bargain and sale to her for one year by force of the statute for transferring uses into possession and assigns forever all that part of a tract called "Cerne Abbey Manor" called "Duddington Manor," "New Troy" and "Duddington Pasture" or whatever name whereon her dwelling house now stands and containing 400 acres. Beginning at the fork of St. James Creek and running along the river to Turkey Buzzard Point. Signed Charles Carroll, Jr., in the presence of John Hepburn, William Elson and acknowledged before John Hepburn

Page 168. At the request of Benjamin Welsh the following Land Commission was recorded abt August 25, 1758
Memorandum that on the special petition of Benjamin Welsh of Anne Arundel County, Maryland preferred to the justices of Prince George's County, Maryland on the 4th Tuesday in November in the 2nd year of his Lordship commission the Right Hon. the Lord Proprietary Dominion etc., his Lordship commission issued by order of the justices aforesaid out of the county aforesaid on the 22nd day of December Anno Domini 1752. In these words following, Frederick Absolute Lord and Proprietary of the Province of Maryland and Avalon Lord Baron of Baltimore vizt; to Messrs Thomas Harwood, James Edmonston, James Crow and Richard Isaac, Jr., of PGCo Gentleman, whereas Benjamin Welsh, is seized of a tract called "Rich Neck" and preferred his petition in writing to our county court held at Upper Marlborough Town before Peter Dent, Gentleman and his associates then and still justices within our county to examine evidence to prove and perpetuate the memory of the bounds of the said tract of land. Therefore, we command you any three or two of you to examine all witnesses or persons concerned touching their knowledge of the bounds of the said tract. Witness Henry Truman, Gentleman, December 6, 1752. Issued December 22, 1752, Joseph Sim, Clk

Notice given to all persons whom it may concern November 22nd to meet the commissioners December 18, 1753, but put off and met on May 6, 1754.

William Davis declares that he was building a tobacco house and at that time came Capt. John Welsh and told him not to set his frame on his land at that time asked him if he knew where the bounded tree stood and the said Davis said yea and pointing to a small fork of the Eastern Branch of Potomack River some distance from them said there stands two bound white oaks and the Capt. John Welsh told him that he supposed them to be the bounded trees of a tract taken up by William Gray which he believes to be the bound tree but was not showed them to be the trees and further saith not. May 6, 1754, William Davis, James Crow, Richard Isaac, Jr.

Mrs. Rachel Welsh of Anne Arundel County, Maryland, declares that as she was riding to their quarter with her husband John Welsh she stopped and said to Isaac Plummer one of William Davis servants why did your master set this frame there for on William Grays land for now you are at work on his land. Tell your master if I don't see him before I go down to come down to me and I will inform him better and further saith not. May 6, 1754, Rachel Welsh, James Crow, Richard Isaac, Jr.

Joseph Cheney declares that Capt. John Welsh told him one day when they were riding together between Welsh's quarter and a small draft on the Eastern Branch and that this is Gray's land and further saith not. May 6, 1754, Joseph Cheney, James Crow, Richard Isaac, Jr.

Mr. Charles Walker, aged 63, declares that his father Charles Walker and Mr. Robert Tyler told him that these were the beginning trees of Rich Neck being two bounded white oaks in the fork of a small draft of the Eastern Branch of Potomack River and they ate their dinners at the said trees and showed me several times the trees and said they were the beginning trees of "Rich Neck" and the bounded trees of Mr. William Gray's land. August 1, 1758, Charles Walker, James Crow, Richard Isaac, Jr.

Page 170. At the request of Ignatius Wheeler the following Deed was recorded August 25, 1758

Indenture made June 8, 1758; between William Hicks, merchant of St. Mary's County, Maryland and Ignatius Wheeler, planter of PGCo. Witnessed that William Hicks by virtue of the award of Messrs Thomas Marshall, Bayne Smallwood and John Stoddert of Charles County, Maryland, Gentlemen, arbitrators indifferently elected and named between the said William Hicks and the parties possessed of 2,400 acres of land part of a tract of 3,000 acres formerly granted to William Calvert Esqr., commonly called "Piscattaway Manor" otherwise "Calvert's Manor," alias "Elizabeth Manor," recovered 1800 acres. Whereas the named Ignatius Wheeler was in possession of 80 acres and hath agreed to purchase of William Hicks the 3/4ths of the same awarded to William Hicks as also William Hicks 3/4ths of 70 acres late in the possession of Christopher Edelen adjoining to the part possessed by Ignatius Wheeler being a tenement whereon Mary Stewart now dwelleth. Beginning at the end of the second course of the manor late in the possession of James Edelen a tenement where Locker Long now dwelleth, from the back line with Richard Edelen's land to the 600 acres land in possession of Thomas Noble and George Noble then to Accokeek Branch and running up to the third course and containing 150 acres. This indenture therefore further witnesseth that William Hicks in consideration of 39 pounds 7 shillings and 6 pence sterling money by Ignatius Wheeler has sold the aforesaid two tracts of land. And further that the said William Hicks will warrant the 3/4ths (112-1/2 acres of the 150 acres). Signed William Hicks in the presence of Robert Hammett, Basil Biscoe and acknowledged before Robert Hammett, James Biscoe, JP's of St. Mary's County, Maryland and at the same time Priscilla Hicks wife of William Hicks relinquished her right of dower

Page 172. At the request of George Gantt the following Deed was recorded August 26, 1758
Indenture made August 23, 1758; John Stevens, planter in consideration of 1 pound 15 shilling sterling paid by George Gantt, Gentleman, has sold part of a tract called "Stevens Adventure" containing 1-3/4 acres and bounded on the west

91

side of Timothy's Branch. Signed John Stevens in the presence of and acknowledged before Thomas Williams, Thomas Contee and at the same time Ellendor Stevens wife of John Stevens relinquished her right of dower

Page 173. At the request of James Marshall the following Deed was recorded August 23, 1758
Indenture made between George Parker, Gentleman of Charles County, Maryland in consideration of 3000 pounds crop tobacco paid by James Marshall, merchant of PGCo has sold part of a lot lying in Piscattaway called "Hazard" which George Parker purchased of Gabriel Parker late of Calvert County, Maryland and Ann Parker his wife by deed enrolled in the year 1743 and containing 1-1/2 acres. Signed George Parker in the presence of and acknowledged before George Gordon, George Gantt

Page 174. At the request of Thomas Hagan the following Deed was recorded August 30, 1758
Indenture made August 26, 1758; Benjamin Notley Mitchell, planter and Tabitha Mitchell his wife, planters in consideration of 1 pound 17 shillings and 10 shillings current money as also two parcels of land called "Widows Trouble" conveyed to me by James Brooke in behalf of Thomas Hagan as satisfaction for land due from said Brooke and for divers other good causes and considerations us thereunto moving have sold unto Thomas Hagan part of a tract of "Widows Trouble" beginning at the north line of said tract laid out by Thomas Blanford for his daughter Tabitha Mitchell containing 57 acres. Signed Benjamin Notley Mitchell, Tabitha Mitchell in the presence of and acknowledged before George Gantt, Thomas Contee and at the same time Tabitha Mitchell wife of Benjamin Notley Mitchell relinquished her right of dower

Page 176. At the request of George Athey the following Certificate of Stray was recorded September 2, 1758
I certify that George Athey, planter, brought before me as a stray a small gray flea bitten horse about 11 hands high and paces.

Athey to keep horse until owner claims. Given under my hand August 28, 1758, George Gordon

Page 176. At the request of Leonard Piles the following Deed was recorded September 2, 1758
Indenture made August 17, 1758; between Francis Piles, planter and Leonard Piles, planter. Witnesseth that whereas Francis Piles did sometime promise and oblige himself to make over unto Leonard Piles part of a tract called "Cuckolds Point" near the Western Branch of Patuxent River formerly bought by his father Francis Piles, deceased of Master Charles Yates for 70 acres which Leonard Piles hath obtained a warrant of resurvey on the whole tract and certified unto the land office the quantity of 56 acres, 41 acres was vacancy added. Now this indenture witnesseth that Francis Piles in consideration of 5 pounds 5 shillings sterling money paid by Leonard Piles has sold part of a tract called "Cuckolds Point" containing 70 acres on the Western Branch of Patuxent River and bounded by "Dear Bought." Signed Francis Piles, Sr. in the presence of and acknowledged before John Campbell, John Bowles and at the same time Sarah Piles wife of Francis Piles relinquished her right of dower

Page 178. At the request of Reverend John Eversfield the following Deed was recorded September 6, 1758
Indenture made September 5, 1758; Thomas Hagan, planter and Margaret Hagan his wife in consideration of 3 pounds Maryland currency and also 1150 pounds of crop tobacco paid by Reverend John Eversfield, clerk, part of a tract called "Widows Trouble" containing 57 acres and beginning at the 9th line of "Widows Trouble" laid out by Thomas Blanford for his daughter Tabitha Notley Mitchell. Signed Thomas Hagan, Margaret Hagan in the presence of and acknowledged before John Hepburn, John Campbell and at the same time Margaret Hagan wife of Thomas Hagan relinquished her right of dower

Page 180. At the request of Richard Jones the following Acknowledgement was recorded September 6, 1758

Deborah Davis, relict of Samuel Davis acknowledged her dower right of the of the within mentioned land to be the right and title of Richard Jones son of Richard Jones. Mordecai Jacob, Thomas Williams

Vide Deed recorded liber JJ folio 187-188

Page 180. At the request of Richard Hutton the following Deed was recorded September 9, 1758

Indenture made August 12, 1758; Jonathan Willson, planter of Frederick County, Maryland in consideration of Richard Hutton making over to George Maxwell all his right and title to a tract called "Hatchet" [sic Lost Hatchett] which was conveyed by John Willson to John Haggarty by which act and deed Jonathan Willson doth acknowledge himself fully satisfied has sold to Richard Hutton all his right title and interest into the remaining part of "Hatchet" which Philip Tattershall conveyed to John Willson beginning in the line of a tract called "Ludford's Gift" and bounded by land formerly belonging to Bernard Johnson and land formerly laid out for Cornelius Canaday. Signed Jonathan Willson in the presence of John Hepburn, Benjamin Berry and acknowledged before John Hepburn and at the same time Martha Willson wife of Jonathan Willson relinquished her right of dower

Page 181. At the request of Isaac Lemaster the following Deed was recorded September 9, 1758

Indenture made September 4, 1758; Jasper Manduit, planter in consideration of 3000 pounds of tobacco paid by Isaac Lemaster, planter has sold a tract called "Scotland" containing 100 acres. Signed Jasper Manduit in the presence of and acknowledged before John Cooke, Christopher Lowndes and at the same time Hannah Manduit wife of Jasper Manduit relinquished her right of dower

Page 183. At the request of John Baynes the following Assignment of Lease was recorded September 9, 1758

We John Sutton, planter and Mary Sutton his wife in consideration of 36 pounds sterling paid by John Baynes,

merchant have assigned and set over by these presents to him all the lands and tenements in Piscattaway called "Hazard" and part of "Never Fear" heretofore demised unto them by John Hawkins, Jr., by a lease bearing date March 25, 1751. To have and to hold said leased land unto John Baynes during the natural lives of the us. In witness whereof we have hereunto set our hands and affixed our seals this September 11, 1758, John Sutton, Mary Sutton in the presence of John Hepburn, Cornelius Davies and acknowledged before John Hepburn, and at the same time Mary Sutton wife of John Sutton relinquished her right of dower to the aforesaid Lease.
Lease recorded in Liber JJ Folio 138-139

Page 183.   At the request of Isaac Brashear the following Certificate of Stray was recorded September 9, 1758
PGCo Sct, September 7, 1758; Isaac Brashear brought before me as trespasser a stray a large sorrel horse branded on the near buttock, shod on his fore feet, several saddle spots. Mordecai Jacob

Page 184.   At the request of John Talburtt the following Certificate of Stray was recorded September 9, 1758
PGCo Sct, September 9, 1758; John Talburtt brought before me a stray mare of strawberry color, has a star and a snip on one of her hind feet, about 12 hands high and he complains she is troublesome and breaks into his inclosures. Christopher Lowndes

Page 184. At the request of Charles Beaven the following Deed was recorded September 13, 1758
Indenture made September 13, 1758; between John Miles and Charles Beaven. Whereas Charles Beaven became bound with John Miles in one bond dated April 4, 1758 to Ignatius Digges for the payment of 87 pounds sterling. Now this indenture witnesseth that John Miles in consideration of securing indemnifying and saving harmless Charles Beaven and for consideration of 5 shillings and for other causes and considerations the said John Miles moving have made over to

95

Charles Beaven Negroes Sarah, Easter, Edward, Robin and Nell, provided that if John Miles shall well and truly indemnify and save harmless Charles Beaven from the payment of the money mentioned in the said bond then this Bill of Sale to be void. Signed John Miles in the presence of John Hepburn, Thomas Brooke and acknowledged before John Hepburn

Page 185. At the request of John Ray, Sr. the following Certificate of Stray was recorded September 19, 1758
Bladensburg, PGCo Sct, September 19, 1758; I do certify that John Ray, Sr., brought before me a stray a small sized black horse with a switch tail, a small white star in the forehead and branded on the off buttock. David Ross

Page 185. At the request of Joseph Peach the following Deed was recorded October 7, 1758
Indenture made September 21, 1758; Charles Carroll, Esqr., of Anne Arundel County, Maryland, in consideration of 5 shillings sterling money of England paid by Joseph Peach, Jr., carpenter of PGCo has sold a tract called "Beaverdam Neck" containing 230 acres and situated on the North East Branch of the Eastern Branch of Potomack River. Signed Charles Carroll, in the presence of and acknowledged before Gilbert Sprigg, John Reresby and at the same time Elizabeth Carroll wife of Charles Carroll relinquished her right of dower

Page 187. At the request of Benjamin Brashear the following Deed was recorded October 7, 1758
Indenture made September 18, 1758; Benjamin Belt, Jr., planter in consideration of 45 pounds Sterling money of Great Britain paid by Benjamin Brashear, planter has sold part of a tract called "Pleasant Hill" containing 150 acres. Signed Benjamin Belt, Jr., in the presence of and acknowledged before Mordecai Jacob, Thomas Williams and at the same time Ruth Belt wife of Benjamin Belt, Jr., relinquished her right of dower

Page 189. At the request of Nacey {Ignatius} Brashear the following Deed was recorded October 7, 1758

96

Indenture made September 18, 1758; Benjamin Belt, Jr., planter in consideration of 45 pounds sterling money of Great Britain paid by Nacey Brashear, planter has sold part of a tract called "Pleasant Hill" containing 115 acres lying on the west side of Still House Branch that falls into the small deep branch of the Eastern Branch of Potomack River. Signed Benjamin Belt, Jr., in the presence of and acknowledged before Mordecai Jacob, Thomas Williams and at the same time Ruth Belt wife of Benjamin Belt, Jr., relinquished her right of dower

Page 191. At the request of Thomas Chittim the following Deed was recorded October 11, 1758
Indenture made September 16, 1758; Jeremiah Crabb, planter and Lucy Crabb his wife, in consideration of 46 pounds 2 shillings currency paid by Thomas Chittim has sold a tract called "Addition to Bacon Hall" containing 100 acres and lying near the head of a branch that runs into the Piney Branch of the Eastern Branch of Potomack River. Signed Jeremiah Crabb, Lucy Crabb in the presence of and acknowledged before Mordecai Jacob, Robert Tyler and at the same time Lucy Crabb wife of Jeremiah Crabb relinquished her right of dower
September 16, 1758; Received of Thomas Chittim 46 pounds 2 shillings currency it being the consideration for the within mentioned land which land was conveyed to me in discharge of so much part of a judgment recovered in the provincial court by the said Thomas Chittim and Thomas Hilleary against the estate of Baruch Williams, deceased. Witnesseth, Jeremiah Crabb, Robert Tyler

Page 193. At the request of Joseph Boarman the following Deed was recorded October 21, 1758
Indenture made June 8, 1758; William Hicks of St. Mary's County, Maryland, merchant in consideration of 39 pounds sterling money paid by Joseph Boarman, planter of PGCo has sold part of a tract lying on Piscattaway Creek, containing 111 acres late in the possession of James Edelen being part of a tract formerly granted to William Calvert Esqr., commonly called "Piscattaway Manor" otherwise "Calvert's Manor," alias

97

"Elizabeth Manor" beginning at a line of the 600 acres in the possession of Thomas Noble and George Noble and bounded by Christopher Edelen's land and 1000 acres of George Noble, deceased. And lastly William Hicks warrants his 3/4ths, i.e. 83-1/4 acres of the above land against all other persons. Signed William Hicks in the presence of Robert Hammett, Basil Biscoe and acknowledged before Robert Hammett, James Biscoe, JP's of St. Mary's County, Maryland and at the same time Priscilla Hicks wife of William Hicks relinquished her right of dower

Page 195. At the request of Joseph Boarman the following Deed was recorded October 21, 1758
Indenture made June 8, 1758; William Hicks of St. Mary's County, Maryland, merchant in consideration of 105 pounds 15 shillings sterling money paid by Joseph Boarman, planter of PGCo has sold part of a tract containing 333 acres late in the possession of William Deakins being part of a tract formerly granted to William Calvert Esqr., commonly called "Piscattaway Manor" otherwise "Calvert's Manor," alias "Elizabeth Manor" beginning in the back line late in the possession of Thomas Noble and bounded by Christopher Edelen's part of the manor and the 600 acres in the possession of Thomas Noble and George Noble. And lastly William Hicks warrants his 3/4ths, i.e. 249-3/4 acres of the above land against all other persons. Signed William Hicks in the presence of Robert Hammett, Basil Biscoe and acknowledged before Robert Hammett, James Biscoe, JP's of St. Mary's County, Maryland and at the same time Priscilla Hicks wife of William Hicks relinquished her right of dower

Page 198. At the request of John Duckett the following Certificate of Stray was recorded October 23, 1758
PGCo Sct, October 23, 1758; This is to certify that John Duckett, planter brought before me as a stray one iron gray mare, about 3 years old, 12 hands high, branded on the near buttock and docked. October 18, 1758, George Gordon

Page 198. At the request of William Deakins the following Deed

98

was recorded October 28, 1758

Indenture made October 10, 1758; Archibald Smith, planter in consideration of 89 pounds, 16 shillings sterling money of Great Britain paid by William Deakins has sold part of a tract called "Edmonton's Pasture" containing 224-1/2 acres. Signed Archibald Smith, in the presence of and acknowledged before David Ross, Thomas Williams and at the same time Mary Smith wife of Archibald Smith relinquished her right of dower

Page 201. At the request of Edward Trafford, Esqr. & Sons the following Bill of Sale was recorded October 28, 1758

I John Dawson, planter in consideration of 1077 pounds of tobacco and 9 pounds 13 shillings and 4 pence currency of Maryland paid by Edward Trafford, Esqr. & Sons, merchants of Liverpool have sold 1 black horse, 2 gray horses, 25 hogs, 2 feather beds with stocks sheets, blankets, quilts or rugs together with all household furniture, 1 cornfield, 1 cart and gears, provided nevertheless that if John Dawson shall well and truly pay unto Edward Trafford, Esqr. & Sons the aforesaid sums with interest on the 1st day of September next then this Bill of Sale to be void. In witness whereof I have set my hand and seal this October 12, 1758, John Dawson in the presence of George Dawson

Page 201. At the request of Henry Scott the following Deed of Gift was recorded October 28, 1758

I Mary Scott, planter in consideration of the natural love and affection which I bear unto my son Henry Scott as for other good causes me hereunto moving have given him Negro woman Clear. To these presents have set my hand and affixed my seal this October 9, 1758, Mary Scott in the presence of Charles Beall, Jeremiah Tannehill

Page 202. At the request of Samuel Pottinger & John Wallingford the following Supersedes was recorded October 28, 1758

You Samuel Pottenger and John Willingsford, William Higgins and William Brashear do confess judgment to James Plummer for the sum of 350 pounds of tobacco which sums were recovered on August 14, 1758 before me one of His Lordships Justices of the Peace to be levied on your goods chattels lands or tenements for the use of James Plummer in case Samuel Pottenger and John Willingsford shall not pay and satisfy the said sum and costs thereon on February 10th next. Thomas Williams, August 14, 1758

Page 202. At the request of Ninian Willett the following Certificate of Stray was recorded November 4, 1758
PGCo Sct, November 4, 1758; I hereby certify that Ninian Willett brought before me a small stray horse about 4 years old, a star in his forehead, the near hind foot white, and branded on the off buttock. August 14, 1758, Joseph Belt, Jr.

Page 202. At the request of William Wheat the following Deed was recorded October [sic November] 6, 1758
Indenture made November 6, 1758; George Naylor, planter in consideration of 30 pounds currency paid by William Wheat have sold a tract called "Smith's Pasture" containing 50 acres and beginning at the south east corner of "Stoke." Signed George Naylor in the presence of and acknowledged before John Hepburn and at the same time Lettice Naylor wife of George Naylor relinguished her right of dower

Page 204. At the request of Stephen West the following Release was recorded November 9, 1758
Indenture made July 27, 1758; Francis Pile, planter in consideration of 30 pounds sterling paid by Stephen West, merchant has sold and released by virtue of a bargain and sale bearing date next before these presents for one whole year for the statue for transferring into Stephen West's possession the following tracts now in his actual possession, "Buck Hill" containing 100 acres originally surveyed for Francis Pile on May 16, 1733 beginning at the south east corner tree of "Maidens Dowry" and bounded by a small branch that runs into St. Charles Branch; also one other tract called "Buck Hills Joyner" originally surveyed for Francis Pile on August 2, 1751

100

containing 40 acres and beginning at "Maidens Dowry" now in the possession of Mr. John Hepburn. Signed Francis Pile, Stephen West in the presence of William Elson, Jeremiah Brashear and acknowledged before John Hepburn

Page 205. At the request of Stephen West the following Lease was recorded November 9, 1758
Indenture made July 26, 1758; Francis Pile, planter in consideration of 5 shillings sterling paid by Stephen West, merchant has sold the following tracts now in his actual possession, "Buck Hill" containing 100 acres originally surveyed for Francis Pile on May 16, 1733 beginning at the south east corner tree of "Maidens Dowry" and bounded by a small branch that runs into St. Charles Branch; also one other tract called "Buck Hills Joyner" originally surveyed for Francis Pile on August 2, 1751 containing 40 acres and beginning at "Maidens Dowry" now in the possession of Mr. John Hepburn. To have and to hold the two tracts from the day next before these presents for and during one whole year for the intent and purpose and of the statute for transferring then into possession of Stephen West. Signed Francis Pile, Stephen West in the presence of William Elson, Jeremiah Brashear

Page 207. At the request of Stephen West the following Deed was recorded November 11, 1758
Indenture made November 11, 1758; between Turnor Wootton, Gentleman and Stephen West, merchant of Upper Marlborough Town. Whereas Benjamin Berry, Sr., inn holder was heretofore committed in the execution to the custody of Turnor Wootton, sheriff and was released by an act of assembly for Insolvent Debtors made at Annapolis in 1755 and whereas Turnor Wootton was empowered to sell and dispose of all the estate and effects of Benjamin Berry for the use of his creditors and whereas Benjamin Berry was possessed of ½ part "Lot Number 14" lying in Upper Marlborough Town (the remaining ½ part the property of Jeremiah Berry on part which the dwelling house of Stephen West now stands) and the same being advertised and sold at public sale to Stephen West for 600

pounds of tobacco. Now this indenture witnesseth that Turnor Wootton in consideration of the 600 pounds of tobacco paid by Stephen West has sold and confirmed unto him "Lot Number 14" lying in Upper Marlborough Town. Signed Turnor Wootton, in the presence of Joh Hepburn, Benjamin Hall son of Francis and acknowledged before John Hepburn

Page 208. At the request of John McGill and John Carrick the following Bill of Sale was recorded November 15, 1758
I John Bullman, planter in consideration of 427 pounds of tobacco and 2 shillings and 6 pence current money paid by John McGill and John Carrick, planters, has sold 1 small sorrel mare, provided nevertheless that I John Bullman will well and truly pay unto Zachariah Lyles the aforesaid sum of money on or before February 10th next then this Bill of Sale to be void. In witness whereof I have set my hand and seal this October 27, 1758, John Bullman in the presence of Mordecai Jacob, Jemima Jacob and acknowledged before Mordecai Jacob

Page 209. At the request of Jane Ellis the following Deed was recorded November 15, 1758
Indenture made January 10, 1758; between William Ellis, school master and widower and Jane Ellis spinster. In consideration of an intermarriage between William Ellis and Jane Ellis to be consummated before the first day of February next, I William Ellis doth make over unto Jane Ellis during the term of her natural life and during the widowhood if William Ellis should die before her, but if she should remarry after his death, then the following estate to descend to the heir of the body of Jane Ellis lawfully begotten and for want of heirs the estate to fall unto Mary Ellis his sister lawfully begotten by George Ellis on the body of Mary Ellis his wife now residents at Milbank in the City of Westminster in the Kingdom of Great Britain, one messuage or tenement lying in Southgate in Middlesex in the Kingdom of Great Britain and late in the tenure of Lady Ann Trevor held at the yearly rent of 25 pounds good lawful money of Great Britain. Provided nevertheless if the said William Ellis or Jane Ellis should refuse to intermarry do bind

102

themselves in the penal sum of 200 pounds of lawful money of Great Britain to be paid within five months after such refusal. Signed William Ellis in the presence of Robert Dove Cook, Jonathan Ellis

Page 210. At the request of John Jenkins the following Lease was recorded November 15, 1758
Indenture made January 2, 1758; Benjamin Tasker, Jr., of ye City of Annapolis as attorney in fact for Thomas Bladen, Esqr., in consideration of the rents and covenants hath demised and to farm let by these presents unto John Jenkins all that tract of land, the property of Thomas Bladen, Esqr., called "Fairfax Beall" containing 200 acres and lying on the Beaver Dam Branch for the term of 21 years paying yearly 800 pounds good merchantable tobacco to be delivered at the Eastern Branch of Potomack River landing in cask on the 25th of March. Further, to plant on the premises before the expiration of 3 years, 100 good apple trees in a regular enclosed orchard. Signed Benjamin Tasker, Jr., John Jenkins in the presence of and acknowledged before Christopher Lowndes, David Ross

Page 211. At the request of Thomas Clark the following Deed was recorded November 15, 1758
Indenture made October 9, 1758; Between Thomas Prindle, planter and Mary Prindle his wife, executrix of the last will and testament of Edward Sprigg, Gentleman, decease and Thomas Clark, Gentleman. Witnesseth that whereas Edward Sprigg did make his last will and testament dated November 30, 1751 and did devise the four following tracts to be sold in one lot at public sale by June 1st next provided they will bring 175 pounds sterling, vizt; "Sprigg's Meadow" containing 183 acres, "The Gore" containing 48 acres, "The Lane" containing 38 acres and "The Addition to The Lane" containing 27 acres. And the same will constituted his wife Mary Sprigg as sole executrix, and as for as Gilbert Sprigg, Gentleman on March 20, 1753 did agree with the said Mary Sprigg for the purchase of the lands at 175 pounds sterling and assigned his right to Thomas Clark. Therefore, they the said Thomas Prindle and Mary Prindle his

103

wife in consideration of 175 pounds sterling paid by Thomas Clark has sold the aforesaid tracts. Signed Thomas Prindle, Mary Prindle in the presence of and acknowledged before John Cooke, Robert Tyler

Page 214. At the request of John Tucker the following Deed was recorded November 24, 1758
Indenture made November 13, 1758; Mary Shircliff, widow in consideration of 5,500 pounds of tobacco clear of casque paid by John Tucker, planter has made over and assigned to him during the natural life of Mr. Walter Hanson of Charles County, Maryland, 1/8th part of a tract lying on the Eastern Branch of Potomack River in PGCo called "The Inclosure" containing 125 acres. Signed Mary Shircliff, in the presence of and acknowledged before Mordecai Jacob, Thomas Williams

Page 215. At the request of William Digges the following Certificate of Stray was recorded March 27, 1758
I hereby certify that David Feithe brought before me a stray small bay gelding with a blaze in his fact, a slender white strip running down to his nose, the near hind foot white and branded on the near buttock. David Ross

Page 215. At the request of John Morris the following Certificate of Stray was recorded November 27, 1758
This is to certify that John Morris has in his possession for this five months past a black stray heifer, 3 years old, neither marked nor branded, a little white under her belly. November 24, 1758, George Gordon

Page 215. At the request of James Watson, Jr. the following Deed was recorded March 29, 1758
Indenture made March 29, 1758; James Watson, Sr., planter in consideration of 22 pounds sterling money of Great Britain paid by James Watson, Jr., has sold part of a tract called "Cole Brooke" containing 100 acres formerly called "Poplar {Hill}" part of "Watson's Forrest." Signed James Watson, in the presence of and acknowledged before John Hepburn, Thomas Lucas

Page 216. At the request of Henry Hilleary the following Deed was recorded December 7, 1758
Indenture made November 13, 1758; William Hilleary, planter in consideration of 90 pounds sterling money paid by Henry Hilleary has sold a tract called "Williams Lot" being part of "Three Sisters" containing 80 acres. Signed William Hilleary in the presence of and acknowledged before Mordecai Jacob, Thomas Williams and at the same time Margaret Hilleary wife of William Hilleary relinquished her right of dower.

Page 218. At the request of John Berry the following Supersedes was recorded December 8, 1758
You John Berry, Alexander Falconar, Jr., and Gilbert Falconar do confess judgment to Thomas Turner for the sum of 28 shillings current money debt and 2 shillings and 6 pence costs which sums were recovered on November 1, 1758 before me one of His Lordships Justices of the Peace to be levied on your goods chattels lands or tenements for the use of Thomas Turner in case John Berry shall not pay and satisfy the said sum and costs thereon on February 10th next. Mordecai Jacob

Page 218. At the request of James Crafts the following Supersedes was recorded December 8, 1758
You James Crafts, Jeremiah Fowler and Able Edwards do confess judgment to Samuel Tannehill for the sum of 18 shillings current money and 150 pounds tobacco debt which sums were recovered on October 23, 1758 before me one of His Lordships Justices of the Peace to be levied on your goods chattels lands or tenements for the use of Samuel Tannehill in case James Crafts shall not pay and satisfy the said sum and costs thereon on February 10th next. Mordecai Jacob

Page 218. At the request of Nathaniel Ryan the following Supersedes was recorded November 28, 1758
You Nathaniel Ryan, William Young and James Gibson do confess judgment to Mr. Turner Wootton for the sum of 349 pounds tobacco and 9 shillings and 6 pence currency which sums were recovered on September 13, 1758 before me one of

His Lordships Justices of the Peace to be levied on your goods chattels lands or tenements for the use of Turner Wootton in case Nathaniel Ryan shall not pay and satisfy the said sum and costs thereon on February 10th next. George Gordon

Page 219.   At the request of John Hinton the following Supersedes was recorded November 28, 1758
You John Hinton, Major Thomas Harwood and Thomas Boyd do confess judgment to Turner Wootton for the sum of 116 pounds tobacco and 5 shillings currency which sums were recovered on September 2, 1758 before me one of His Lordships Justices of the Peace to be levied on your goods chattels lands or tenements for the use of Turner Wootton in case John Hinton not pay and satisfy the said sum and costs thereon on February 10th next. Robert Tyler

Page 219.   At the request of John Brashear the following Supersedes was recorded November 28, 1758
You John Brashear, William Duckett and Paul Rankin do confess judgment to James Beck, Jr., for the sum of 1 pound 15 shillings and 6 pence currency which sums were recovered before me one of His Lordships Justices of the Peace to be levied on your goods chattels lands or tenements for the use of James Beck, Jr., in case John Brashear shall not pay and satisfy the said sum and costs thereon on February 10th next. Robert Tyler

Page 219.   At the request of George McCalley the following Supersedes was recorded November 30, 1758
You George McCalley, John Wells and John Brown do confess judgment to Walter Phelps for the sum of 2 pounds 9 shillings and 6 pence debt and cost of warrant which sum was recovered on November 23, 1758 before me one of His Lordships Justices of the Peace to be levied on your goods chattels lands or tenements for the use of Walter Phelps in case George McCalley shall not pay and satisfy the said sum and costs thereon on February 10th next. Robert Tyler

Page 220. At the request of George Naylor & Lettice Naylor the

following Deed was recorded November 28, 1758
Indenture made September 19, 1758; between Thomas Lawson, planter and George Naylor and Lettice Naylor his wife, planters and after their decease to John Lawson Naylor. Witnesseth that Thomas Lawson in consideration whereof the said Thomas Lawson doth hereby confess and acknowledge hath granted unto George Naylor and Lettice Naylor his wife and after their decease to their son John Lawson Naylor a tract containing 100 acres and bounded by "Woodbridge." Signed Thomas Lawson in the presence of John Hepburn, Samuel Northey and acknowledged before John Hepburn

Page 221. At the request of John Beall son of Robert the following Deed was recorded November 29, 1758
Indenture made November 22, 1758; Thomas Plummer, planter of Frederick County, Maryland in consideration of 40 pounds currency paid by John Beall son of Robert, planter of PGCo, has sold part of a tract called "William & Elizabeth" containing 100 acres. Signed Thomas Plummer in the presence of John Darnall, Thomas Hagan and acknowledged before John Darnall (JP of Frederick County, Maryland) and at the same time Rachel Plummer wife of Thomas Plummer relinquished her right of dower

Page 223. At the request of Elizabeth Mullikin the following Bill of Sale was recorded November 30, 1758
Indenture made November 13, 1758; James Mockbee in consideration of 18 pounds 10 shillings sterling and 794 pounds of inspected tobacco paid by Elizabeth Mullikin, Negro Jane. Nevertheless if James Mockbee shall well and truly pay unto Elizabeth Mullikin the aforesaid sums of money and tobacco before November 13, 1759 then this obligation and sale to be void. Signed James Mockbee, in the presence of and acknowledged before Joseph Belt, Jr.

Page 224. At the request of William Bowie the following Land Commission was recorded abt November 30, 1758
Memorandum that on the special petition of William Bowie

preferred to the justices of Prince George's County, Maryland on the 4th Tuesday in March in the 8th year of his Lordship commission the Right Hon. the Lord Proprietary Dominion etc., his Lordship commission issued by order of the justices aforesaid out of the county aforesaid on the 21st day of April Anno Domini 1758. In these words following, Frederick Absolute Lord and Proprietary of the Province of Maryland and Avalon Lord Baron of Baltimore vizt; to Messrs Robert Bradley, Thomas Hollyday, Samuel Roundell and William Deakins of PGCo Gentleman, whereas William Bowie, is seized of a tract called "Brooke Point" and preferred his petition in writing to our county court held at Upper Marlborough Town before Joseph Belt, Jr., Gentleman and his associates then and still justices within our county to examine evidence to prove and perpetuate the memory of the bounds of the said tract of land. Therefore, we command you any three or two of you to examine all witnesses or persons concerned touching their knowledge of the bounds of the said tract. Witness Joseph Belt, Jr., Gentleman, April 10, 1758. Issued April 21, 1758, Joseph Sim, Clk

Pursuant to a commission to examine evidences to prove the bounds of "Brooke Point" we hereby give notice that we intend to meet at the lands on Wednesday, June 24th day of this month. Witness our hands and seals this May 3, 1758, Samuel Roundell, Robert Bradley, Thomas Holliday

PGCo September 23, 1758; The affirmation of Mr. James Brooke of Frederick County, Maryland, Quaker, aged about 53 years declares that a large white oak near where is a stone placed standing near a spring branch and about 100 yards to the east of the Chapel that his father and his uncle John Brooke that the said oak was the north east corner tree of "Brooke Point" and a bounded tree of Goughs land now in the possession of Daniel Page. On the same day we went to a marked hickory standing about 60 yards from a ditch, and James Brooke declared that his father and his uncle John Brooke that the said hickory was the 6th tree of "Brooke Reserve" and standing in the line of "Brooke Point and a bounded tree of Gough's land aforesaid and further saith not. James Brooke, Robert Bradley, Samuel Roundell, Thomas Holliday

Page 225. At the request of Samuel Turner the following Land Commission was recorded abt November 30, 1758

Memorandum that on the special petition of Samuel Turner preferred to the justices of Prince George's County, Maryland on the 4th Tuesday in June in the 8th year of his Lordship commission the Right Hon. the Lord Proprietary Dominion etc., his Lordship commission issued by order of the justices aforesaid out of the county aforesaid on the 24th day of August Anno Domini 1758. In these words following, Frederick Absolute Lord and Proprietary of the Province of Maryland and Avalon Lord Baron of Baltimore vizt; to Messrs Thomas Williams, Jeremiah Belt, Jr., Thomas Chittam and Mordecai Jacob of PGCo Gentleman, whereas Samuel Turner, is seized of a tract called "Yarrow" and preferred his petition in writing to our county court held at Upper Marlborough Town before Joseph Belt, Jr., Gentleman and his associates then and still justices within our county to examine evidence to prove and perpetuate the memory of the bounds of the said tract of land. Therefore, we command you any three or two of you to examine all witnesses or persons concerned touching their knowledge of the bounds of the said tract. Witness Joseph Belt, Jr., Gentleman, June 30, 1758. Issued August 24, 1758, Joseph Sim, Clk

Advertisement, Pursuant to an order to examine evidences to prove the bounds of "Yarrow" we hereby give notice that we intend to meet at the dwelling house of said Turner on Tuesday, October 10th next. Witness our hands and seals this May 15, 1758, Thomas Williams, Jeremiah Belt, Jr., Mordecai Jacob and Thomas Chittam

We met agreeable to Advertisement and from thence to the west side of the Eastern Branch of Potomack River about 1-1/2 miles above said Turner's plantation to three marked gum, where;

William Prather, aged 58 years declares about 30 years ago or upwards he saw an oak either red or black in that place that appears to him to be a fair bounded tree and took it as the beginning tree of "Yarrow." And further saith that some years after he saw the aforesaid tree dead and the top broke off that he went to James Edmonston and told him that his beginning tree was dead and the said Edmonston took little or no notice and sometime after on the east side of the aforesaid branch opposite to this deponents house James Edmonston had two sawyers at work and he asked him if his land came so far on the high ground and he told him, this deponent, that his line came nigh the road and further sayeth not. From thence we went to the east side of the Eastern Branch of Potomack River and 100 yards from the branch to a marked gum where;

Col. Joseph Belt aged 78 declares that 30 odd years ago he was a commissioner to perpetuate the bounds of a tract called "Friendship" belonging to Col. Addison and there was a dispute between him and Capt. Archibald Edmonston concerning "Yarrow" and that it run with "Friendship" three lines and further saith not.

John Banks aged 81 years declares that about 35 years ago there was a commissioner to prove the bounds of "Friendship" and this deponent was present and there was a dispute between Col. Addison and Capt. Archibald Edmonston about their lands called "Friendship" and "Yarrow" and that he saw a marked water oak or Spanish oak near the aforesaid gum and at that time some of the company asked Capt. Archibald Edmonston if that was his bounded tree and he answered no and said his beginning tree stood over the branch looking to the westward, and then asked so you run to the "Friendship" and he said yes and accordingly the did begin at the aforesaid Spanish oak and run three lines. This deponent being asked if he knew whether Capt. Archibald Edmonston claimed this Spanish oak for his bound tree he says no and further sayeth not. We adjourned to ye November 8th to the aforesaid Spanish oak.

John Beall aged 48 years says in 1753 at the request of Andrew Beall, I run part of Capt. Archibald Edmonston land from a marked gum which we are now at and some short time after I was with him in the woods above his plantation where we were talking about the lands in dispute between him and Andrew Beall and after we had gone some small distance we came to a place where I had run a line of the said Edmonston's land I then showed him the place, [and] he told me we were wrong and asked me where I had run from [and] I told him from a marked gum which was shown to me to be a corner tree of Abington's land. He said the place should be the end of my line of Abington's land and that place is the end of the first line of my land. And I said I believe there is not a man living who knows the beginning tree of my land that the youths are mistaken and I will let them know it some day and sometime after I was at Mr. Edmonston's house and he told me I had run into his land near to a spring which is not far from the place that Capt. Edmonston had told him before that he was wrong and further saith not.

Archibald McDonald, aged 35 years declares that about 6 years ago Capt. Joshua Beall was running "Friendship" and Capt. James Edmonston was with them and says near this gum they stopped and Capt. Joshua Beall and Mr. Scott asked Mr. Edmonston to let them borrow here on this level for fear of running into the Eastern Branch and Mr. Edmonston said no for it will make a great deal of difference to borrow on level land and pay upon hilly ground for his land run a great many courses with the "Friendship" and further saith not. Thomas Williams, Mordecai Jacobs, Jeremiah Belt, Jr., Thomas Chittam

Page 228. At the request of Archibald McDonald the following Land Commission was recorded abt November 30, 1758

Memorandum that on the special petition of Archibald McDonald preferred to the justices of Prince George's County, Maryland on the 4th Tuesday in March in the 7th year of his Lordship commission the Right Hon. the Lord Proprietary Dominion etc., his Lordship commission issued by order of the justices aforesaid out of the county aforesaid on the 21st day of April Anno Domini 1758. In these words following, Frederick Absolute Lord and Proprietary of the Province of Maryland and Avalon Lord Baron of Baltimore vizt; to Messrs Thomas Williams, Thomas Chittam, Jeremiah Belt, Jr. and William Prather of PGCo Gentleman, whereas Archibald McDonald, is seized of a tract called "Friends Goodwill" and preferred his petition in writing to our county court held at Upper Marlborough Town before Joseph Belt, Jr., Gentleman and his associates then and still justices within our county to examine evidence to prove and perpetuate the memory of the bounds of the said tract of land. Therefore, we command you any three or two of you to examine all witnesses or persons concerned touching their knowledge of the bounds of the said tract. Witness Joseph Belt, Jr., Gentleman, April 10, 1758. Issued April 21, 1758, Joseph Sim, Clk

By Virtue of a commission to examine evidences to prove the bounds of "Friends Goodwill" we hereby give notice that we intend to meet at the lands on Wednesday August 16th next. Witness our hands and seals this July 24, 1758, Thomas Williams, Thomas Chittam, Jeremiah Belt, Jr. and William Prather

On August 16, 1758 we met as advertised and proceeded to a burnt stump which appeared to us to be lately cut down and burnt standing northward of Archibald McDonald's plantation near a marked box oak where;

John Banks aged 81 years or thereabouts declared that James Lee showed him this tree and told him it was his beginning tree and Capt. Edmonston showed him the tree and said it was the beginning tree of James Ford's land and further saith not.

Archibald Edmonston aged 51 or thereabouts declared that being employed to survey "Friends Goodwill was carried to a bounded white oak by James Lee the employer and after the some courses being run, James Edmonston came to me and said what was done was wrong and he took us to another tree and said that was the right tree and further saith not.

Joseph Peach, Jr., aged 27 or thereabouts declares that his father was empowered to run the land about 7-8 years ago and he run from this said tree being informed by James Edmonston that this was the right tree and further this deponent sayeth not.

Joseph Peach, Sr., aged upwards of 65 years or thereabouts declares that James Ford in his lifetime gave him the courses of the land in order to plot and run it round for him and beginning at a bounded white oak standing near a line of "Friendship" and further told this deponent that Mr. James Edmonston (now deceased) advised him to take up this land {same as James Ford} and further Mr. Edmonston ordered where the courses of the land should run which civility occasioned the land to be called "Friends Goodwill and further this deponent says some few years since that John Mitchell now deceased employed him to run out "Friends Goodwill" for James Lee and then this deponent sent to Mr. James Edmonston desiring him to come and shew the beginning. He returned that he was very sick and could not come but gave directions how and where it might be easily to be found same as James Ford} which said boundary myself and the rest of the company soon found and further saith not. From thence we went done the hill to a white oak in the line of the main road and Archibald McDonald's plantation.

David Mitchell declares 12-13 years ago Thomas Butts shewed him this tree and told him it was the beginning tree of "Friends Goodwill" and that he was shewd it by James Ford who was the taker up of this land and that the said Mitchell sold the said land from this tree to James Leigh and further sayeth not.

John Riddle aged 57 or thereabouts declares that 8 years ago James Leigh (best to his memory) shewd him a white box oak tree near the burnt stump and further saith not.

Thomas Webb aged 55 or thereabouts declares that 8-9 years ago John Camble carried him to the above tree and told him it was the beginning tree of "Friends Goodwill" and that James Lee shewed him the said tree then carried him to the tree that John Riddle had just sworn to and further saith not. We adjourned to the 23rd said month where;

James Ford aged 38 years or thereabouts declares he heard his father say that it run on the side of the hill facing a bottom next to the plantation where Archibald McDonald now lives and that he heard his uncle Thomas Prather say it look in the bottom from the first running and further sayeth not. Jeremiah Belt, Jr., Thomas Chittam

Page 231. At the request of Samuel Luckett the following Land Commission was recorded abt November 30, 1758

Memorandum that on the special petition of Samuel Luckett preferred to the justices of Prince George's County, Maryland on the 4th Tuesday in November in the 7th year of his Lordship commission the Right Hon. the Lord Proprietary Dominion etc., his Lordship commission issued by order of the justices aforesaid out of the county aforesaid on the 17th day of

December Anno Domini 1757. In these words following, Frederick Absolute Lord and Proprietary of the Province of Maryland and Avalon Lord Baron of Baltimore vizt; to Messrs William Young, Walter Evans, John Beall, joyner and James Wight of PGCo Gentleman, whereas Samuel Luckett, is seized of a tract called "Seaman's Delight" and preferred his petition in writing to our county court held at Upper Marlborough Town before Joseph Belt, Jr., Gentleman and his associates then and still justices within our county to examine evidence to prove and perpetuate the memory of the bounds of the said tract of land. Therefore, we command you any three or two of you to examine all witnesses or persons concerned touching their knowledge of the bounds of the said tract. Witness Joseph Belt, Jr., Gentleman, December 2, 1757, Joseph Sim, Clk

By virtue of a commission to examine evidences to prove the bounds of "Seaman's Delight" lying on the north side of the Eastern Branch of Potomack River we hereby give notice that we intend to meet at the dwelling plantation of Samuel Luckett on Tuesday, April 25th next. Witness our hands and seals this March 9, 1758, William Young, Walter Evans

PGCo Sct, August 12, 1758; In pursuant of a commission perpetuating the memory of the bounds of "Seaman's Delight" lying on the north side of the Eastern Branch of Potomack River we hereby give notice that we intend to meet at the dwelling plantation of Samuel Luckett on Monday, September 25th next. William Young, Walter Evans

April 25, 1758, John Flint aged 68, at a bounded white oak standing on the north side and near the mouth of a small branch that runs into the Eastern Branch deposes that about 30 years ago he run "Seaman's Delight" for Col. Bradford and several times since always ran from the aforesaid tree for the beginning of the land.

Adam Miller aged 73 deposes that his father George Miller showed him the aforesaid white oak for the beginning tree of "Seaman's Delight" and "Barbadoes," that his father settled and lived for many years.

John Flint the above deponent being at an old red oak about 100 yards from the road that leads from Bladensburg to

Georgetown on the west side opposite to where Abraham Lemaster now lives deposes that Col. Bradford showed him the aforesaid oak for the uppermost tree of "Seaman's Delight" and that he saw proved as such.

Adam Miller the above deponent being at the aforesaid red oak deposes that he heard Col. Bradford say it was the uppermost tree of "Seaman's Delight" and further say he saw John Dekons/Deakins proven to be the uppermost tree and the second tree of "Barbadoes"

John Wight aged 44 deposes that about 22 years ago Capt. Charles Beall since deceased went with him to a place on a hill where a small box white oak is bounded about 80 yards from the main road that leads from Bladensburg to Georgetown against the head of three springs and told him there did stand an old black oak which was then down which was a tree of Hyde's land that Mme. Bradford then lived on and a tree of Queen's land and Richard Marsham Waring since deceased showed him the aforesaid tree about two months afterward for a tree of "Seaman's Delight" and "The Inclosure" and said that they run from 500 perches to a small hickory down by the marsh and this deponent further saith about 13 years ago Thomas Lucas since deceased brought him to the aforesaid place and said there stood a tree of "Seaman's Delight" which was a tree of "Cuckolds Delight," a tree of Sprigg's land and a tree of "The Inclosure." And this deponent understood it to be the third tree of "Seaman's Delight" and that it ran 500 perches to a small hickory by Ashford's Gutt.

John Wight being at a marked hickory standing near the marsh on the lower side of Ashford's Gutt that runs into the Eastern Branch deposes that the aforesaid Thomas Lucas showed him where a white oak stood near the aforesaid hickory and told him it was the last tree of "Seaman's Delight" and that he saw Capt. Charles Beall and Walter Evans prove it to be a tree of the aforesaid land and the tree of "The Inclosure" and that "Haddock's Hills" lay above

May 30, 1758; Adam Miller aged 73 being at a box oak formerly marked with two notches standing at the head of the most northerly valley that leads down on the south side where the deponent formerly lived deposes that between 30-40 years ago William Smith then owner of "Seaman's Delight" had the aforesaid land run in came near the aforesaid tree with the end of the first line but was not certain of the spot.

Robert White aged 83 years and being 80 yards eastward of the box oak mentioned in the deposition of Adam Miller deposes that 30 odd years ago Col. Bradford got "Seaman's Delight" of William Smith and that they run the said land in the first line and ended near where the deponent then was and that and running the lines they came near where Adam Miller then lived and that he called to him the aforesaid Miller to come and see himself righted but that he did not come.

Robert White being at a black oak mentioned in the aforesaid deposition of John Flint and Adam Miller deposes that he saw John Dekone/Deakins prove it to be a tree of 100 acres of land that he bought of Ashford or Col. Bradford but of which she does not remember and that would it was a part of the land called "Haddock's Hills."

September 25, 1758; John Wight aged 45 being at an old red oak east of a small box oak described in the former deposition of Adam Miller deposes on August 6th last Joseph Lord since deceased came with him to the aforesaid tree and told him it was a corner tree of "Barbadoes" that he was shown it by his wife, Col. Bradford, Adam Miller and several others. Thomas Sanders asked Lord which side of the land lay and he showed them to the east that he saw run by Mr. Stoddart and they entered not far from the tree and Lord declared the reason he had for coming with them was that he was very ailing and seemed desirous that the tree should be known and that he should not live to see it proved.

Thomas Sanders aged 32 years deposes that he came to the aforesaid tree in company with Joseph Lord and John Wight and that Lord said it was a corner tree of "Barbadoes" and that he was shown it by his wife, Col. Bradford, Adam Miller and several others. He asked Lord which side of the land lay and he showed them to the east. Given under our hands and seals William Young, Walter Evans

Page 235. At the request of Elizabeth Batt the following Land Commission was recorded abt November 30, 1758

Memorandum that on the special petition of Elizabeth Batt preferred to the justices of Prince George's County, Maryland on the 4th Tuesday in March in the 6th year of his Lordship commission the Right Hon. the Lord Proprietary Dominion etc., his Lordship commission issued by order of the justices aforesaid out of the county aforesaid on the 2nd day of April Anno Domini 1757. In these words following, Frederick Absolute Lord and Proprietary of the Province of Maryland and Avalon Lord Baron of Baltimore vizt; to Messrs Thomas Waring, Thomas Chittam, Thomas Hilleary and James Willson of PGCo Gentleman, whereas Elizabeth Batt, is seized of a tract called "Elizabeth" and preferred his petition in writing to our county court held at Upper Marlborough Town before Peter Dent, Gentleman and his associates then and still justices within our county to examine evidence to prove and perpetuate the memory of the bounds of the said tract of land. Therefore, we command you any three or two of you to examine all witnesses or persons concerned touching their knowledge of the bounds of the said tract. Witness Joseph Belt, Jr., Gentleman, March 26, 1757. Joseph Sim, Clk

By virtue of a commission to examine evidences to prove the bounds of "Elizabeth" we hereby give notice that we intend to meet at the lands on Thursday, September 15th next. Witness our hands and seals this August 4, 1757.

William Dent aged 27 or thereabouts declares that some time ago William Beall, Jr., came with Mr. Samuel Beall and himself and pointed to the ground where we now stand about 20 yards to the eastward of the northwest branch of the Eastern Branch of Potomack River and near a marked dogwood tree where formerly stood a bounded beech the beginning tree of "Elizabeth" or "St. Elizabeth" formerly exposed to sale by Mr. Notley Rozier by way of a lottery and further saith not given under our hands and seal this September 20, 1757 Thomas Hilleary, Thomas Chittam

Page 237. At the request of Thomas Selby the following Land

Commission was recorded abt November 30, 1758

Memorandum that on the special petition of Thomas Selby preferred to the justices of Prince George's County, Maryland on the 4th Tuesday in June in the 8th year of his Lordship commission the Right Hon. the Lord Proprietary Dominion etc., his Lordship commission issued by order of the justices aforesaid out of the county aforesaid on the 10th day of July Anno Domini 1758. In these words following, Frederick Absolute Lord and Proprietary of the Province of Maryland and Avalon Lord Baron of Baltimore vizt; to Messrs William Deakins, Dorsett Hoye, Hilleary Lyles and James Pelley of PGCo Gentleman, whereas Thomas Selby, is seized of a tract called "Essex Lodge" and preferred his petition in writing to our county court held at Upper Marlborough Town before Joseph Belt, Jr., Gentleman and his associates then and still justices within our county to examine evidence to prove and perpetuate the memory of the bounds of the said tract of land. Therefore, we command you any three or two of you to examine all witnesses or persons concerned touching their knowledge of the bounds of the said tract. Witness Joseph Belt, Jr., Gentleman, June 30, 1758. Issued July 10, 1758, Joseph Sim, Clk

By virtue of a commission to examine evidences to prove the bounds of "Essex Lodge" we hereby give notice that we intend to meet at the lands on 23rd of this instant. Witness our hands and seals this September 2, 1758 William Deakins, Dorsett Hoye, Hilleary Lyles

William Magruder Selby aged 49 years in regards to the bounds of a tract of land called "Essex Lodge" now in possession of Thomas Selby declares about 30 years ago Maj. John Bradford and his father William Selby both deceased told him that a white oak tree where is now fixed a cedar post on a small hill near the marsh and about 150 yards on the south of John Selby's dwelling house was the beginning tree of "Essex Lodge" and likewise the beginning tree of a tract called "Leith" and further saith not. William Magruder Selby, William Deakins, Dorsett Hoye

William Magruder Selby aged 49 years at a black oak tree on the south side of the road that goes from John Selby's by William

Scott's declares that about 30 years ago Maj. John Bradford and his father William Selby both deceased told him that the aforesaid tree was the beginning of the dividing line of "Essex Lodge" between Maj. John Bradford's and William Selby and further saith not. William Magruder Selby, William Deakins, Dorsett Hoye

William Magruder Selby aged 49 being at a place between where he dropped a stake on the north side of an old rolling road that went down to Mattapany Creek landing and about 160 yards from Thomas Hodgkin's dwelling house declares about 30 years ago Maj. John Bradford and his father William Selby both deceased told him it was the end of the dividing line of "Essex Lodge" between Maj. John Bradford and William Selby and further saith not. William Magruder Selby, William Deakins, Dorsett Hoye

Page 239.   At the request of William Dove the following Certificate of Stray was recorded November 19, 1758
I hereby certify that this day William Dove, Jr., brought before me as a trespasser and stray a dark bay mare branded on the near thigh, a white speck on her forehead. December 23, 1758, Thomas Williams

Page 239.   At the request of James Moore the following Certificate of Stray was recorded December 16, 1758
PGCo Sct, December 16, 1758; James Moore brought before me a dark bay stallion about three years old and 11 hands high, not branded and complains that he is troublesome and breaks into his enclosures. Christopher Lowndes

Page 239.   At the request of Hilleary Lyles the following Certificate of Stray was recorded December 20, 1758
I hereby certify that Hilleary Lyles brought before me a small black mare taken up as a stray, unbroke has a small star and is branded on the near buttock. December 20, 1758, Joseph Belt, Jr.

Page 239. At the request of William Magruder the following

Deed was recorded December 21, 1758
Indenture made December 8, 1758; Nathaniel Magruder, planter in consideration of 30 pounds sterling money paid by William {Mills} Magruder, planter has sold all his right title and interest which he bought of William Eaglin to two parts of a tract called "Vale of Benjamin" containing 60 acres. Signed Nathaniel Magruder in the presence of and acknowledged before Mordecai Jacob, Robert Tyler

Page 240. At the request of Charles Carroll the following Mortgage was recorded December 21, 1758
We Lancelot Wilson and Richard Cheney jointly and severally in consideration of five shillings sterling paid by Charles Carroll, Esq. as well as for securing unto the said Charles Carroll, Esq. of the sum of 267 pounds sterling now due unto him have sold the Negroes, Frank and Harry the property of Richard Cheney and Negroes Cate, Peg, Alsey, Jack and Janney the property of Lancelot Wilson. Provided nevertheless that if Lancelot Wilson and Richard Cheney shall well and truly pay unto Charles Carroll, Esq. the aforesaid sum of money and interest from the date of the date hereof then this present Bill of Sale to be void. In witness whereof we have hereunto set our hands and seals this December 15, 1758, Lancelot Wilson Richard Cheney in the presence of Robert Croxall, John Kersby and acknowledged before John Brice

Page 241. At the request of Charles Carroll the following Bill of Sale was recorded December 21, 1758
I Orlando Smith in consideration of five shilling sterling paid by Charles Carroll, Esq. as well as for securing unto Charles Carroll the sum of 50 pounds sterling now due unto him have sold by these presents has sold Negro Essex. Provided nevertheless that if Orlando Smith shall well and truly pay unto Charles Carroll the aforesaid sum of money and interest from the day of the date hereof then this present Bill of Sale to be void. In witness whereof I have set my hand and seal this December 15, 1758, Orlando Smith in the presence of Robert Croxall, John Kersby and acknowledged before John Brice

Page 242. At the request of Basil Magruder the following Deed was recorded December 21, 1758
Indenture made November 30, 1758; Robert Soper, Jr., planter in consideration of 25 pounds sterling money paid by Basil Magruder has sold part of a tract called "Batson's Vineyard" containing 50 acres. Signed Robert Soper, Jr., in the presence of John Hepburn, Richard Smith and acknowledged before John Hepburn

Page 243. At the request of Elisha Lanham the following Deed was recorded December 23, 1758
made December 6, 1758; John Lanham, Sr., planter out of the love and affection that he hath and doth bear unto his son Elisha Lanham and five shillings has given part of two tracts "Dickerson's Lott" and "Foxes Hole" containing 96 acres. Signed John Lanham, Sr., in the presence of and acknowledged before John Cooke, Robert Tyler

Page 244. At the request of Nathaniel Magruder the following Deed was recorded December 23, 1758
Indenture made December 8, 1758; William Magruder, planter in consideration of 30 pounds sterling money paid by Nathaniel Magruder has sold part of a tract called "Turkey Cock Branch" being part of "Vale of Benjamin" now called "Beall's Purchase" containing 52 acres and beginning at the northwest corner trees of tracts "Alexandria" and "Dublin" and bounded by the southwest corner tree of "Vale of Benjamin," William Lowe's land, Turkey Branch and Maureen Duvall's land. Signed William Magruder in the presence of and acknowledged before Mordecai Jacob, Robert Tyler and at the same time Mary Magruder wife of William Magruder relinquished her right of dower

Page 247. At the request of Joseph Simpson the following Deed was recorded December 23, 1758
Indenture made December 13, 1758; John Parmer and Mary Parmer his wife in consideration of 6000 pounds of tobacco paid by Joseph Simpson has sold a tract called "Two Johns"

containing 100 acres and beginning at the first bound tree of "Lanham's Folly" and bounded by Thomas Lanham, Jr., land. Signed John Parmer, Mary Parmer in the presence of John Hepburn, Elisha Lanham and acknowledged before John Hepburn and at the same time Mary Parmer wife of John Parmer relinquished her right of dower

Page 247. At the request of Charles Runnolds the following Certificate of Stray was recorded January 13, 1759
This is to certify Charles Runnolds brought before me as a stray a black horse about 12-½ hands high, a large white star in his forehead, a switch tail and branded on the off buttock. George Gordon

Page 247. At the request of Enoch Magruder the following Bill of Sale was recorded January 13, 1759
I William Hilleary, planter in consideration of 45 pounds 12 shillings sterling money of Great Britain paid by Enoch Magruder, merchant have sold Negro Dick and Young Dick. Provided that if William Hilleary shall well and truly pay unto Enoch Magruder the aforesaid sum of money upon the first day of June 1760 then this indenture to be void. In witness whereof I have set my hand and seal this December 26, 1758, William Hilleary in the presence of and acknowledged before Thomas Williams

Page 248. At the request of Tobias Belt the following Certificate of Stray was recorded January 13, 1759
I certify that Tobias Belt brought before me a stray bay horse branded on the near thigh, has three white feet, a star in his forehead and saddle spots on each side. January 10, 1759, Thomas Williams

Page 249. At the request of Joseph Clark the following Certificate of Stray was recorded January 16, 1759
PGCo Sct, January 13, 1759; Joseph Clark brought before me a stray gray mare, neither branded nor docked appears to be about five years old. George Gantt

122

Page 249.   At the request of John Watson the following Certificate of Stray was recorded January 16, 1759
PGCo Sct, January 13, 1759; John Watson brought before me a stray small bay mare branded on the near buttock. George Gantt

Page 249.   At the request of Margaret Hilleary the following Certificate of Stray was recorded January 21, 1759
PGCo Sct, January 19, 1759; I hereby certify that Margaret Hilleary brought before me a small bay horse taken up as a stray, branded on the off buttock, a small star in his forehead and about 3-4 years old. Joseph Belt Jr.

Page 249.   At the request of James Prather the following Certificate of Stray was recorded March 29, 1758
PGCo Sct, March 27, 1758; James Prather brought before me a small mare of a mouse color no visible brand a large star in her forehead complains she is troublesome and breaks into his enclosures. Christopher Lowndes

Page 249. At the request of John Clagett the following Deed was recorded January 27, 1759
Indenture made January 20, 1759; Edward Clagett, planter in consideration of 25 pounds sterling money of Great Britain paid by John Clagett, planter and for divers other good causes and considerations hereunto moving has sold a tract called "Greenland" which land was formerly conveyed to Edward Clagett by Richard Clagett contained 200 acres and beginning on the side of Cabin Branch and the fourth bounded tree of "Greenland." Signed Edward Clagett in the presence of John Hepburn, Allen Bowie and acknowledged before John Hepburn

Page 251. At the request of John Clagett the following Bill of Sale was recorded January 27, 1759
I Edward Clagett, planter in consideration of 20 pounds sterling money of Great Britain paid by John Clagett, planter have sold by these presents Negro Charles (7-9 yrs.) In witness whereof I have set my hand and seal this January 20, 1759, Edward Clagett in the presence of John Hepburn, Allen Bowie and

acknowledged before John Hepburn

Page 251. At the request of Thomas Athey the following Certificate of Stray was recorded January 31, 1759
Thomas Athey brought before me a grey mare branded on the off buttock and her right hind foot is white. George Gantt

Page 251. At the request of Alice Clark & Margaret Lee Clark the following Deed was recorded February 1, 1759
Indenture made January 17, 1759; Thomas Clark, Gentleman in consideration of the love and affection which he hath and beareth unto Alice Clark widow of Thomas Clark, Jr. and Margaret Lee Clark his grandchild as also for the better maintenance and also for divers other good causes and considerations him thereunto moving has given by these presents a tract called "Backland" containing 300 acres for the term of her natural life and after her decease to the use of Margaret Lee Clark and for default of such issue to the said Thomas Clark. Signed Thomas Clark in the presence of John Hepburn, Richard Smith and acknowledged before John Hepburn

Page 252. At the request of Benjamin Belt, Jr., the following Certificate of Stray was recorded January 31, 1759
I certify that Benjamin Belt, Jr., brought before me as a trespasser and stray a young large black roan horse no brand, shod before and has a star in his forehead. Thomas Williams

Page 252. At the request of James Green the following Deed was recorded March 1, 1759
Indenture made March 1, 1758; John Thompson son and heir of Thomas Thompson, planter in consideration of 10,000 pounds of tobacco paid by James Green, Sr., planter has sold a part of a tract called "Providence" that lies on the south side of Stoddert's new road, also part of a tract called "Aix" it being a moiety of the land willed by James Green, deceased to his daughter Elizabeth Thompson. Signed John Thompson in the presence of John Hepburn, Benjamin Brookes and acknowledged before John

Hepburn and at the same time Sarah Thompson wife of John Thompson relinquished her right of dower

Page 253. At the request of Samuel Scott the following Certificate of Stray was recorded February 1, 1759
PGCo Sct, January 30, 1759; Samuel Scott, brought before me a small bay mare as a trespasser and stray with two hind white feet, a blaze in her face, no brand. Mordecai Jacob

Page 253. At the request of Joseph Boarman the following Deed was recorded February 10, 1759
Indenture made November 29, 1758; William Deakins, planter in consideration of 35 pounds six shillings and six pence sterling money paid by Joseph Boarman has sold part of the land lying in Prince George's County, Maryland containing 333 acres late in the occupation of Zachariah Wade and Anne Wade his wife being part of a tract of land formerly granted to William Calvert, Esq., commonly called Piscattaway Manor, otherwise "Calvert's Manor" (alias Elizabeth Manor) beginning being the end of the first course of a part of the manor late the occupation of Thomas Noble and bounded by Christopher Edelen's part of the manor and the 600 acres in possession of Thomas Noble and George Noble. And the said William Deakins by these presents covenant grant and agreed to with the said Joseph Boarman that 1/4th of the above-mentioned land which is 83 ¼ acres, that Joseph Boarman forever hereafter shall and may quietly and peaceably have hold and possess and enjoy the above said parcel and shall have all the right title property to the other three fourths of the above-mentioned land. Signed William Deakins In the presence of and acknowledged before Thomas Williams, Thomas Contee and at the same time Tabitha Deakins wife of William Deakins relinquished her right of dower

Page 255. At the request of John Bowling the following Deed was recorded January 10, 1759
Indenture made December 19, 1758; Joseph Boarman, planter of PGCo, in consideration of 17 pounds 13 shillings sterling money paid by John Bowling, carpenter of Charles County,

Maryland has sold part of the land lying in Prince George's County, Maryland containing 175 acres formerly granted to William Calvert, Esq., commonly called Piscattaway Manor, otherwise "Calvert's Manor" (alias Elizabeth Manor) beginning at a bounded chestnut standing at the head of Pocket Branch at the Church Spring. Signed Joseph Boarman In the presence of and acknowledged before Thomas Williams, Thomas Contee and at the same time Mary Boarman wife of Joseph Boarman relinquished her right of dower

Page 256. At the request of Benjamin Berry, Jr. the following Deed was recorded February 10, 1759
Indenture made February 3, 1759; Robert Bradley, Gentleman in consideration of 100 pounds sterling money of Great Britain paid by Benjamin Berry, Jr., inn holder has sold "Lot Number 4" lying in Upper Marlborough Town excepting that part which Robert Bradley the father of the aforesaid Robert Bradley sold to Capt. Thomas Clagett and now in the possession of David Craufurd. Signed Robert Bradley in the presence of John Hepburn, Richard Smith and acknowledged before John Hepburn

Page 257. At the request of Nathaniel Barker the following Certificate of Stray was recorded February 12, 1759
Nathaniel Barker brought before me a large black mare taken up as a stray, she is branded on the off buttock, some white in her forehead and several white spots on her back. February 8, 1759, George Gantt

Page 258. At the request of Basil Waring the following Deed was recorded February 14, 1759
Indenture made December 15, 1758; Fielder Powell of North Carolina, widow and Osborn Powell of North Carolina, eldest brother of William Powell late of Carolina deceased but now both being in Prince George's County Maryland and in consideration of 41 pistoles paid by Basil Waring, Gentleman has sold part of a tract called "St. Andrews" formerly the dwelling plantation of William Powell containing 150 acres.

Signed Fielder Powell, Osborn Powell in the presence of and acknowledged before J. Sprigg, Joseph Belt Jr.

Page 259. At the request of Benjamin Truman the following Supersedes was recorded February 17, 1759
You Benjamin Truman, James Collings and James Watson, Jr., do confess judgment to Violetta Smith for the sums of 43 shillings and 10 pence half penny currency debt and 10 shillings and 2 shillings and 6 pence currency costs which sums were recovered on December 21, 1758 to be levied on your goods chattels lands or tenements for the use of Violetta Smith in case Benjamin Truman shall not pay and satisfy the said sum and costs thereon on February 10th next. Thomas Contee

Page 259. At the request of Benjamin Hall the following Deed was recorded February 17, 1759
Indenture made January 19, 1758 [sic 9]; Benjamin Duvall (Marsh) in consideration of 60 pounds sterling money of Great Britain paid by Benjamin Hall has sold part of a tract called "Pleasant Grove" containing 482 acres. Signed Benjamin Duvall (Marsh) in the presence of and acknowledged before Mordecai Jacob, Robert Tyler and at the same time Mary Duvall wife of Benjamin Duvall relinquished her right of dower

Page 261. At the request of Richard Hutton the following Agreement was recorded February 17, 1759
Memorandum, it is agreed between betwixt Col. Allen Davies of Charles County, Maryland and Richard Hutton Prince George's County, Maryland. Whereas Richard Hutton has now depending two actions of ejectment before the provincial court for one tract of land in Prince George's County now in possession of the said Allen Davies, part of "Ludford's Gift." Now in consideration Richard Hutton has agreed to drop the said actions and not to proceed any further in the attachments until such time as John Perrie heir at law to the said land arrives to the full age of 21 years and Allen Davies hereby obliges himself to pay to Richard Hutton all legal costs and charges concerning the ejectment and whatever tobacco Richard Hutton has already been paid which

is computed to be about 1000 pounds weight Allen Davies obliges himself to make it equal to whatever price, gave this year. In witness whereof these presents are subscribed this August 22, 1758, Allen Davies.

Witness; Thomas Brouster (Brewster), George Maxwell

{mm: John Perrie son of Samuel Perrie d. 1744 and Margaret Smith who remarried Allen Davies}

Page 261. At the request of Henry Lowe the following Deed was recorded February 17, 1759

Indenture made February 17, 1759; John Lowe, planter in consideration of 14 pounds sterling paid by Henry Lowe, inn keeper has sold a tract called the "Inclosure" lying in St. Mary's County, Maryland containing 75 acres and bounded by Weeklife {Wickliffe now called Wheatley} Creek, Coopers Creek and David Hoult's land. Signed John Lowe in the presence of John Hepburn, Benjamin Berry and acknowledged before John Hepburn

Page 262. At the request of Richard Brooke the following Deed was recorded February 19, 1759

Indenture made August 22, 1758; between Dr. William Lyon of Baltimore County, Maryland and Richard Brooke executor of Mr. Isaac Brooke, late of PGCo, Gentleman. Witness whereas Henry Darnall, Jr., Gentleman and Rachel Darnall his wife by their indenture of lease bearing date July 26, 1754 did farm let unto William Sim, merchant, a tract called "Brookefield" containing 333 acres and adjoining to the plantation of Mrs. Jane Contee for the term of 21 years. Now this indenture further witness that whereas by the death of William Sim the right of the demised premises is in William Lyon. Therefore the said William Lyon in consideration of 147 pounds sterling paid by Isaac Brooke in his lifetime on August 6, 1752, assigns forever by these presents to Richard Brooke executor of Isaac Brooke all the estate right title terms of year claim and demand whatever which he William Sim had by the indenture of lease. Signed William Lyon in the presence of and acknowledged before Ruxton Gay, William Rogers

Page 263. At the request of Joseph Perry the following Certificate of Stray was recorded February 19, 1759
PGCo Sct, February 16, 1759; I certify that Joseph Perry, brought before me as a trespasser and stray a small gray mare, she has no perceivable brand, and small black spots on her head. Thomas Williams

Page 264. At the request of William Hamilton the following Lease was recorded February 24, 1759
Indenture made January 18, 1759. Thomas Lancaster in consideration of the rents and covenants here in after reserved has demised and to farm let by these presents unto William Hamilton one moiety or part of an acre of land adjoining to Queen Anne Town and at the northwest corner of "Tyler's Lott," containing and laid out for 8232 ft. square to have and to hold for the term of 21 years paying yearly unto Thomas Lancaster 10 shillings sterling money of Great Britain. Signed Thomas Lancaster in the presence of Richard Shipley, William Turner Wootton and acknowledged before Mordecai Jacob, Robert Tyler

Page 265. At the request of John Wood the following Certificate of Stray was recorded February 24, 1759
PGCo, February 23, 1759; this day John Wood brought before me a small dun mare taken up as a stray, branded on the near shoulder and buttock's, has a blaze in her face and three white feet, been lately trimmed and is with foal. George Gantt

Page 265. At the request of Basil Magruder the following Certificate of Stray was recorded February 26, 1759
I hereby certify that Mr. Basil Magruder brought before me a small stray yellow color dun horse, a small blaze in his face, bob tail but no perceivable brand. February 27, 1759, J. Sprigg

Page 265. At the request of Charles Beall the following Certificate of Stray was recorded March 3, 1759
I hereby certify that Charles Beall on the Eastern Branch brought before me horse taken up as a stray of a mouse color

13 hands high appears six years old, trots and gallops, is branded imperfectly on the near buttock, the off hind foot white and a large star an a small snip. Joseph Belt, Jr., March 3, 1759

Page 265. At the request of Thenable Edwards the following Certificate of Stray was recorded March 8, 1759
PGCo Sct, March 5, 1759; Thenable Edwards brought before me as a trespasser and stray a middle size sorrel mare with a star in her forehead, her right hind foot white no perceivable brand and black colt with a blaze face, four white feet neither branded or direct docked, a small black mare with a small star in her forehead, her right ear cropt no perceivable brand. Mordecai Jacob

Page 265. At the request of Henry Lowe the following Deed was recorded March 10, 1759
Indenture made March 10, 1759; Andrew Abington, Gentleman in consideration of 45 pounds current money of the province paid by Henry Lowe, innkeeper has sold a tract called "Carrick Fergus" containing 181 acres and bounded by Mr. Wade's land called "Friendship," Kisconko Creek, and "Locust Thickett" formerly the lands of Randolph Hinson. To have and to hold the said parcel excepting that part of the tract taken up by Francis Coffer recovered by a commission on the land and now in possession of Edward Clarkson which remaining part containing 100 acres belonging unto the said Henry Lowe. Signed Andrew Abington in the presence of John Hepburn, William Elson and acknowledged before John Hepburn

Page 267. At the request of Sarah Isaac the following Deed was recorded March 10, 1759
Mordecai Jacob in consideration of the natural love and affection I do bear unto my sister Sarah Isaac, wife of Richard Isaac, Jr. and other good and weighty considerations me hereunto moving have given by these presents all that tract lately belonging to my father Benjamin Jacob called "Jacob's Hope" containing 100 acres on the North branch of Patuxent River between where Thomas Turner and William Ducker now

lives. Signed Mordecai Jacob in the presence of and acknowledged before Thomas Williams, Robert Tyler and at the same time Jemima Jacob wife of Mordecai Jacob relinquished her right of dower

Page 267. At the request of Thomas Brooke, Jr. the following Lease was recorded March 13, 1759
Indenture made March 13, 1759; between Dr. Richard Brooke executor of Isaac Brooke late of PGCo County deceased and Thomas Brooke, Jr. witnessed that whereas Henry Darnall, Jr. and Rachel Darnall his wife by their indenture of lease bearing date July 26, 1750 did demise and to farm let unto William Sim, merchant of tract called "Brookefield" containing 333 acres and adjoining to the plantation of Mrs. Jane Contee for the term of 21 years and whereas by the death of William Sim the right of the aforesaid demised premises was vested in William Lyon of Baltimore County, Maryland administrator of William Sim and afterwards William Sim by his indenture bearing date August 6, 1752 did in consideration of the sum of 147 pounds sterling paid by Isaac Brooke in his lifetime did thereby discharge the said Isaac Brooke and did after the decease of the said Isaac Brooke sell and set over unto Richard Brooke executor of Isaac Brooke deceased all the estate right title and interest in the unexpired term of years which William Sim had. Now this indenture further witness that Richard Brooke executor of Isaac Brooke in consideration of 250 pounds currency paid by Thomas Brooke, Jr. has sold the aforesaid tract of "Brookefield" for the unexpired term of years remaining. Signed Richard Brooke in the presence of John Hepburn, Richard Smith and acknowledged before John Hepburn

Page 269. At the request of Jeremiah Berry the following Deed was recorded March 17, 1759
Indenture made October 19, 1758; Josias Beall, Jr in consideration of 535 pounds sterling money paid by Jeremiah Berry has sold parts of tracts called "Beall's Adventure (alias Good Luck)," "Fathers Gift," "Rovers Content" and "The Inclosure" containing 750 acres. Signed Josias Beall, Jr. in the

presence of and acknowledged before Nathaniel Magruder, George Gantt

Page 271. At the request of Basil Burgess the following Certificate of Stray was recorded March 24, 1759
PGCo Sct, March 19, 1759; I hereby certify that Basil Burgess brought before me a small bay mare taken as a stray marked with a star and two white feet behind, no perceivable brand and appears 8-10 years old. Joseph Belt, Jr.

Page 271. At the request of Zachariah Wade the following Deed of Gift was recorded March 29, 1759
I Mary Wade in consideration of the love goodwill and affection which I have and do bear towards my son Zachariah Wade have given forever part of a tract called "Stoney Harbor" containing 250 acres beginning at a bounded white oak standing near Tinker's Run; also a tract called "Wades Adventure" containing 100 acres. In witness whereof I have hereunto set my hand and seal this March 20, 1759, Mary Wade in the presence of and acknowledged before Thomas Williams, Nathaniel Magruder

Page 273. At the request of Henry Humphrey the following Mortgage was recorded March 29, 1759
Indenture made March 28, 1759; Charles Robinson, shipwright in consideration of 100 pounds paper current money of the province paid by Henry Humphrey has sold Negroes Harry, Nan, Terry, Jim, Will, George, Moll, Patt, London and Ginny; provided that the said Charles Robinson shall well and truly pay unto Henry Humphrey the aforesaid sum of money on or before March 21, 1761 then these presents shall be void. Signed Charles Robinson in the presence of John Hepburn, William Shaw and acknowledged before John Hepburn

Page 273. At the request of James Smith the following Land Commission was recorded abt March 29, 1759
Memorandum that on the special petition of James Smith preferred to the justices of Prince George's County, Maryland on the 4th Tuesday in June in the 8th year of his Lordship

commission the Right Hon. the Lord Proprietary Dominion etc., his Lordship commission issued by order of the justices aforesaid out of the county aforesaid on the 10th day of July Anno Domini 1758. In these words following, Frederick Absolute Lord and Proprietary of the Province of Maryland and Avalon Lord Baron of Baltimore vizt; to Messrs Samuel White, James Draine, Abraham Woodward and John Bateman of PGCo Gentleman, whereas James Smith, is seized of a tract called "Thorpland" and preferred his petition in writing to our county court held at Upper Marlborough Town before Joseph Belt, Jr., Gentleman and his associates then and still justices within our county to examine evidence to prove and perpetuate the memory of the bounds of the said tract of land. Therefore, we command you any three or two of you to examine all witnesses or persons concerned touching their knowledge of the bounds of the said tract. Witness Joseph Belt, Jr., Gentleman, June 30, 1758. Issued July 10, 1758, Joseph Sim, Clk

Pursuant to a commission to examine evidences to prove the bounds of "Thorpland" we hereby give notice that we intend to meet at the lands on Saturday, March 24th. Witness our hands and seals this March 3, 1759, Samuel White, Abraham Woodward and John Bateman

William Brashear, Sr., aged about 50 years declares about 20 years ago he was present when Mr. Peter Dent was employed by his uncle Samuel Brashear to run "Thorpland" beginning at a gum which he saw proved by Nathaniel Wickham, Sr., Samuel Brashear and Benjamin Brashear, Sr., and running to a bounded white oak the second tree of the tract standing on the west side of a hill and east side of Collington Branch and this deponent further saith not. November 16, 1758, Samuel White, John Bateman and Abraham Woodward

March 24, 1759; Thomas Wood, Sr., aged 63 years declares about 33-35 years ago John Demald [sic Demall] showed me the second tree of Brock's land and run from it and said upon that hill there stood a tree of John Brown's land called "Thorpland" and further saith not. Samuel White, John Bateman and Abraham Woodward

Page 275. At the request of Edward Boteler the following Land Commission was recorded abt March 29, 1759

Memorandum that on the special petition of Edward Boteler preferred to the justices of Prince George's County, Maryland on the 4th Tuesday in March in the 7th year of his Lordship commission the Right Hon. the Lord Proprietary Dominion etc., his Lordship commission issued by order of the justices aforesaid out of the county aforesaid on the 21st day of April Anno Domini 1758. In these words following, Frederick Absolute Lord and Proprietary of the Province of Maryland and Avalon Lord Baron of Baltimore vizt; to Messrs William Eversfield, John Dorsett, William Dorsett and William Deakins of PGCo Gentleman, whereas Edward Boteler, is seized of a tract called "Essex Lodge" and preferred his petition in writing to our county court held at Upper Marlborough Town before Joseph Belt, Jr., Gentleman and his associates then and still justices within our county to examine evidence to prove and perpetuate the memory of the bounds of the said tract of land. Therefore, we command you any three or two of you to examine all witnesses or persons concerned touching their knowledge of the bounds of the said tract. Witness Joseph Belt, Jr., Gentleman, April 16, 1758. Issued April 21 1758, Joseph Sim, Clk

Advertisement, by virtue of a commission to examine evidences to prove the bounds of "Essex Lodge" we hereby give notice that we intend to meet at the lands on Wednesday, July 5th next. Witness our hands and seals this June 3, 1758, William Eversfield, John Dorsett, William Newman Dorsett

John Orme, Sr., aged 68 years declares that about 50 years ago Col. Ninian Beall, deceased told him that a black gum tree standing on the south east side of a hill where now is placed a large stone was a corner tree of "Essex Lodge" now in the possession of Charles Boteler, Sr., and further saith not. William Eversfield, John Dorsett, William Newman Dorsett

Page 276. At the request of Benjamin Truman the following Land Commission was recorded abt March 29, 1759

Memorandum that on the special petition of Benjamin Truman preferred to the justices of Prince George's County, Maryland on the 4th Tuesday in March in the 6th year of his Lordship commission the Right Hon. the Lord Proprietary Dominion etc., his Lordship commission issued by order of the justices aforesaid out of the county aforesaid on the 4th day of April Anno Domini 1757. In these words following, Frederick Absolute Lord and Proprietary of the Province of Maryland and Avalon Lord Baron of Baltimore vizt; to Messrs Alexander Magruder, George Biggs, Thomas Morton and Thomas Letchworth of PGCo Gentleman, whereas Benjamin Truman, is seized of two tracts called "Thomas & Anthony Choice" and "Blackwell" and preferred his petition in writing to our county court held at Upper Marlborough Town before Peter Dent, Gentleman and his associates then and still justices within our county to examine evidence to prove and perpetuate the memory of the bounds of the said tracts of land. Therefore, we command you any three or two of you to examine all witnesses or persons concerned touching their knowledge of the bounds of the said tract. Witness Joseph Belt, Jr., Gentleman, March 26, 1757. Issued April 4, 1757, Joseph Sim, Clk

Pursuant to a commission to examine evidences to prove the bounds of "Thomas & Anthony Choice" and "Blackwell" we hereby give notice that we intend to meet at the lands on Thursday, Jan 11th next. Witness our hands and seals this December 19, 1758, Alexander Magruder, Thomas Morton, Thomas Letchworth

James Fry aged 40 years or thereabouts declares about 30 years ago his father Joseph Fry had begun to cut down the hickory where he now stands. It was a notch tree he left off and sometime after Mr. Edward Truman to whom the land at that time did belong told this deponent's father it was his bound tree and at that time his father was tenant to Edward Truman but did not remember the name of the land it belong to and this deponent further saith not. Alexander Magruder, Thomas Morton, Thomas Letchworth

Page 278. At the request of Henry Smith Hawkins the following Land Commission was recorded abt March 29, 1759
Memorandum that on the special petition of Henry Smith

Hawkins preferred to the justices of Prince George's County, Maryland on the 4th Tuesday in June in the 8th year of his Lordship commission the Right Hon. the Lord Proprietary Dominion etc., his Lordship commission issued by order of the justices aforesaid out of the county aforesaid on the 14th day of September Anno Domini 1758. In these words following, Frederick Absolute Lord and Proprietary of the Province of Maryland and Avalon Lord Baron of Baltimore vizt; to Messrs John Lowe, Henry Lowe, Alexander Norton and Benjamin Musgrove of PGCo Gentleman, whereas Henry Smith Hawkins, is seized of a tract called "Batchelors Harbour" and preferred his petition in writing to our county court held at Upper Marlborough Town before Joseph Belt, Jr., Gentleman and his associates then and still justices within our county to examine evidence to prove and perpetuate the memory of the bounds of the said tract of land. Therefore, we command you any three or two of you to examine all witnesses or persons concerned touching their knowledge of the bounds of the said tract. Witness Joseph Belt, Jr., Gentleman, August 25, 1758. Issued September 14, 1758, Joseph Sim, Clk

We the subscribers being duly qualified according to the law and by advertisement having giving timely notice according to the act of assembly in such cases made and provided did on March 6, 1759 repair and to the boundaries of "Batchelors Harbour" and then and there took the following depositions;

John Hanson aged 49 years or thereabouts declared that about nine or 10 months ago James Robinson showed him a cedar stump where he now stands on the mouth of the St. George's Creek and told him it was the first bound tree of a tract called Batchelors Harbour and further saith not

Charles Robinson age 36 or thereabouts declares that his father James Robinson told him that a cedar stump standing on the mouth of St. George's Creek was a bounded tree of the "Neck Land" and further saith not

John Robinson aged 28 years or thereabouts declares at the cedar stump where he now stands his father told him that it was a bound tree of the "Neck Land" and further saith not

William Davis aged 40 years or thereabouts declares that this red oak where we now are on the mouth of Jerome Creek is the second bound tree of "Batchelors Harbour" and he was told by some persons as was present at the running of the land that it was the second tree of the said land, Mr. John Smith and Mr. Thomas Hodgkin the surveyor being present and run the land and further saith not. Alexander Norton, Benjamin Musgrove

Page 279. At the request of Nicholas Davis, Jr. the following Land Commission was recorded abt March 29, 1759
Memorandum that on the special petition of Richard Hutton preferred to the justices of Prince George's County, Maryland on the 4th Tuesday in March the 7th year of his Lordship commission the Right Hon. the Lord Proprietary Dominion etc., his Lordship commission issued by order of the justices aforesaid out of the county aforesaid on the 21st day of April Anno Domini 1758. In these words following, Frederick Absolute Lord and Proprietary of the Province of Maryland and Avalon Lord Baron of Baltimore vizt; to Messrs Thomas Brooke, Jr., Benjamin Brooke, William Eversfield and George Naylor of PGCo Gentleman, whereas Nicholas Davis, Jr., is seized of tracts called "Little Grove" and "Ward's Purchase" and preferred his petition in writing to our county court held at Upper Marlborough Town before Joseph Belt, Jr., Gentleman and his associates then and still justices within our county to examine evidence to prove and perpetuate the memory of the bounds of the said tracts of land. Therefore, we command you any three or two of you to examine all witnesses or persons concerned touching their knowledge of the bounds of the said tracts. Witness Joseph Belt, Jr., Gentleman, April 13, 1758. Issued April 21, 1758, Joseph Sim, Clk
By virtue of a commission to examine evidences to prove the bounds of "Little Grove" and "Ward's Purchase" we hereby give notice that we intend to meet at the lands on Thursday, August 10th next. Witness our hands and seals this July 1, 1758, Thomas Brooke, Benjamin Brooke, William Eversfield
Bartholomew Fields age 45 years or thereabouts says that about 20 years ago or thereabouts Murphy Ward deceased told him that a black oak standing in the fork of two branches near

137

the main road that leads to Piscattaway was a bounded tree of Thomas Wall, deceased land.   Thomas Brooke, Benjamin Brooke, William Eversfield

Page 280.   At the request of John Hill the following Land Commission was recorded abt March 29, 1759
Memorandum that on the special petition of John Hill preferred to the justices of Prince George's County, Maryland on the 4th Tuesday in August in the 8th year of his Lordship commission the Right Hon. the Lord Proprietary Dominion etc., his Lordship commission issued by order of the justices aforesaid out of the county aforesaid on the 4th day of December Anno Domini 1758. In these words following, Frederick Absolute Lord and Proprietary of the Province of Maryland and Avalon Lord Baron of Baltimore vizt; to Messrs John Cooke, Thomas Williams, Nathaniel Offut and Nathaniel Magruder of PGCo Gentleman, whereas John Hill, is seized of a tract called "Baltimore" and preferred his petition in writing to our county court held at Upper Marlborough Town before Joseph Belt, Jr., Gentleman and his associates then and still justices within our county to examine evidence to prove and perpetuate the memory of the bounds of the said tract of land. Therefore, we command you any three or two of you to examine all witnesses or persons concerned touching their knowledge of the bounds of the said tract. Witness Joseph Belt, Jr., Gentleman, December 1, 1758. Issued December 1, 1758, Joseph Sim, Clk
Advertisement, in pursuance to a commission to examine evidences to prove the bounds of "Baltimore" we hereby give notice that we intend to meet at the lands on Thursday, February 15th next. Witness our hands and seals this December 29, 1758, John Cooke, Thomas Williams, Nathaniel Magruder, Nathaniel Offutt
James Tannehill aged 53 being sworn at a bounded white oak tree standing in the fork of the cattail marsh that he has his hand on 27 or 28 years ago he was present when Walter Evans and William Tannyhill on oath in his hearing prove the above white oak tree to be the first bounded tree of Mr. Clement Hills land and that it was then proved on a land commission taken out by

the said Clement Hill and further saith not. John Cooke, Nathaniel Magruder

Philip Evans aged 64 years being sworn at a gum tree standing on cleared ground to the westward of Mr. Thomas Waring's dwelling house saith that 27 or 28 years ago he was present when Walter Evans and William Tannyhill on oath in his hearing prove the above gum tree to be the second bound tree of Mr. Clement Hill's land and that it was then proved on the land commission taken out by Clement Hill and further saith not. John Cooke Nathaniel Magruder

Philip Evans aged 64 years deposes at a bounded dead white oak tree standing on the edge of the low grounds adjoining Cabin Branch that about 27 or 28 years ago when Mr. Clement Hill had a land commission to prove the bounds of his land at the same time Mr. Tannyhill said in the hearing of him that the next course of the land from the tree went down the branch and further this deponent says not. John Cooke Nathaniel Magruder

James Tannyhill aged 53 years deposeth at a bounded white oak tree standing in the edge of the low grounds of adjoining Cabin Branch that he was present 27 or 28 years ago when Walter Evans and William Tannyhill proved the above white oak to be the third bound tree of Mr. Clement Hill's land and further saith not. John Cooke, Nathaniel Magruder

Benjamin Berry aged 63 years deposeth at a bounded dead white oak tree standing in the edge of the low grounds of adjoining Cabin Branch he was a commissioner 27 or 28 years ago on a land commission taken out by Clement Hill when Walter Evans proved the aforesaid tree. John Cooke, Nathaniel Magruder

Philip Evans aged 64 years deposes at a bounded white oak tree standing in the fork of cattail marsh that 27 or 28 years ago he was present when Walter Evans and William Tannyhill on oath in his hearing prove the aforesaid white oak tree to be the first bounded tree of Mr. Clement Hills land and that it was then proved on a land commission taken out by the said Clement Hill and further saith not. John Cooke, Nathaniel Magruder

Page 282. At the request of Ignatius Digges & Walter Hoxton the

following Assignment was recorded March 28, 1759
I Theodore Contee, attorney in fact for Hancock Lee late of PGCo, merchant in consideration of 114 pounds 14 shillings and eight pence sterling being the consideration money and interest paid by Ignatius Digges, Esq. and Walter Hoxton of PGC has sold and assigned two tracts of land and Negroes and all other the premises with the appurtenances in and by the mortgage granted to Hancock Lee. In witness whereof I have hereunto set my hand and seal this March 30, 1759, Theodore Contee in the presence of Joseph Sim

Page 282. At the request of Nathaniel Ranter the following Deed was recorded March 30, 1759
Indenture made November 17, 1758; Thomas Finch, planter in consideration of 5000 pounds of inspected tobacco in one pounds sterling money paid by Nathaniel Ranter, planter has sold a tract called "The Forrest" containing 100 acres originally granted to Thomas Brooke, Esq. on August 16, 1695 together with the vacancy of 19 acres added by a resurvey be made by Thomas Hodgkin deputy surveyor on November 15, 1754. Beginning at a marked sampling by the main road that leads from Mattapany to the Wood Yard. Thomas Finch in the presence of John Hepburn, Joseph Yates and acknowledged before John Hepburn and at the same time Ann Finch wife of Thomas Finch relinquished her right of dower

Page 284. At the request of Thomas Gordon the following Certificate of Stray was recorded March 30, 1759
I hereby certify that on March 24, 1759 was brought before me by Thomas Gordon bay mare taken up as a stray about 12 hands high, no brand, more than a little white above the foot of and her off hind foot, hanging mane and a large switch tail and appears to be 7 years old, trots and gallops. John Cooke

Page 284. At the request of James Wardrop the following Deed was recorded March 31, 1759
Indenture made March 31, 1759; John Hepburn, Esq. in consideration of 50 pounds sterling money of Great Britain paid

140

by James Wardrop, merchant has sold all that moiety or part of a tract called "Horse Pen" formerly purchased by Patrick Hepburn, physician deceased of Dinah Ayre, widow by deed bearing date April 29, 1726 and according to the metes and bounds expressed in a deed from James Moore to Thomas Box bearing date February 15, 1700. Signed John Hepburn in the presence of and acknowledged before Joseph Belt, Jr., John Cooke

Page 285. At the request of Lewis Duvall the following Deed was recorded April 10, 1759
Indenture made March 15, 1759; David Mitchell, planter of Frederick County, Maryland in consideration of 50 pounds current money of Maryland paid by Lewis Duvall, planter of PGCo, has sold parts of two adjoining tracts called "Tyler's Pasture" and "Mitchell's Addition" containing 129 acres. Signed David Mitchell in the presence of and acknowledged before Mordecai Jacob, Robert Tyler and at the same time Mary Mitchell wife of David Mitchell relinquished her right of dower

Page 287. At the request of Thomas Marshall the following Deed was recorded abt April 10, 1759
Indenture made 1759; James Edelen, Gentleman of PGCo in consideration of 15 pounds sterling paid by Thomas Marshall of Charles County, Maryland has sold part of a tract first taken up by James [sic William] Calvert, Esq. known by Calvert's Manor being one fourth of that in that part conveyed by deed of bargain from William Hicks of St. Mary's County, Maryland to Thomas Marshall by deed bearing date June 8, 1758. Beginning in Accokeek Main Branch containing 170 acres. Signed James Edelen in the presence of John Hepburn, William Elson and acknowledged before John Hepburn and at the same time Salome Edelen wife of James Edelen relinquished her right of dower

Page 289.   At the request of Jonathan Throne Sasser the following Deed of Gift was recorded April 16, 1759
I John Sasser for divers good causes and weighty considerations

me hereunto moving have given by these presents to unto my loving son Jonathan Throne Sasser Negro boy James. By virtue here of I have hereunto set my hand and seal this April 11, 1759, John Sasser in the presence of William Ellis, Richard Gray

Page 289. At the request of James Truman Greenfield the following Mortgage was recorded April 16, 1759
I Gerard Truman Greenfield, Gentleman of PGCo in consideration of 110 pounds current money paid by James Truman Greenfield of St. Mary's County, Maryland has sold six Negroes; Rachel, Pegg, Miel, Fidow, Darby being part of the increase of the said Rachel and Negro Doll. Provided nevertheless that if Gerard Truman Greenfield shall well and truly pay unto James Truman Greenfield the aforesaid sum of money with legal interest at or upon March 31, 1761 then this Bill of Sale to be void. Gerard Truman Greenfield in the presence of John Chesley, Nathaniel Truman Greenfield and acknowledged before John Chesley

Page 290. At the request of Elizabeth Sasser the following Deed of Gift was recorded April 16, 1759
I John Sasser, chaulker, for diverse good causes and weighty considerations me hereunto moving has given by these presents unto my loving daughter Elizabeth Sasser Negro boy David. By virtue here of I have hereunto set my hand and seal this April 11, 1759; John Sasser in the presence of William Ellis, William Watson

Page 291. At the request of Lewis Duvall the following Bill of Sale was recorded April 16, 1759
I James Gore, planter of Frederick County, Maryland in consideration of 105 pounds current money paid by Lewis Duvall have sold Mulatto man James (28 yrs.) and Negro Sal (30 yrs.). In witness whereof I have set my hand and seal this December 23, 1758, James Gore in the presence of John Orme, John Ray, Jr.

Page 291. At the request of Verlinda Orme wife of Moses Orme,

142

Jr., Priscilla Taylor, Ann Taylor & Susannah Taylor daughters & Coheirs of Samuel Taylor the following Release of mortgage was recorded April 16, 1759

We Francis Waring of PGCo and George Parker of Charles County, Maryland in consideration that we have been saved and kept harmless by Samuel Taylor in his lifetime and by Mary Taylor administratrix of Samuel Taylor and from the bonds bearing date September 17, 1744 which we Francis Waring, George Parker and John Lawson with the said Samuel Taylor did become jointly and severally bound for the only debt of Samuel Taylor unto Mary Sim of PGCo, widow in the sum of 66,000 pounds of tobacco conditioned for the payment of 33,000 pounds of good sound clean tobacco and 33 hogshead's clear of wood at some convenient landing on Patuxent River for the redemption of all that part of land lying in PGCo whereupon Samuel Taylor then lived called "Taylorton" containing 240 acres and one adjoining tract called "Taylors Pasture" containing 38 ½ acres and bounded on the south side by Taylors Creek. As also Negro girl Kate, 5 horses, 3 mares, 20 black cattle and sheep which he lately mortgaged to us of the said Francis Waring and George Parker have survived for the keeping and saving us harmless for the eight several bonds aforesaid. And we do confess that by keeping and saving us harmless that all our interests right title property is clearly and absolutely extinguished and that Verlinda Orme wife of Moses Orme, Jr., Priscilla Taylor, Ann Taylor and Susannah Taylor daughters and coheirs of Samuel Taylor is of the lands aforesaid seized and possessed to the use of them. In witness whereof we have set our hands and seal this March 13, 1759, Francis Waring, George Parker and in the presence of and acknowledged before Robert Tyler, Thomas Williams

Page 293. At the request of Peter Robinson the following Indenture was recorded April 16, 1759

Indenture made January 5, 1759; John Healy, planter regarding the interest and well-being of his daughter Mary Ann Healy age 12 years the 15th day of this instant January and he being truly sensible of his own inability to maintain support and educate

143

his daughter during her minority does hereby bind her unto Peter Robinson, school master and Ann Robinson his wife until she arrived to the age of 16 years. Signed John Healy, Peter Robinson in the presence of and acknowledged before John Hepburn

Page 294. At the request of David Burnes the following Certificate of Stray was recorded March 26, 1759
I certify that David Burnes by his son James Burns brought before me a stray a small dark bay gelding, about 12 hands high, marked on the near buttock, has a white star in the face. March 26, 1759, David Ross

Page 294. At the request of Thomas Strickland the following Certificate of Stray was recorded April 16, 1759
PGCo Sct, April 13, 1759; Thomas Strickland brought before me as a trespasser and stray a small bay mare a star in her forehead branded on the near shoulder. Mordecai Jacob

Page 294. At the request of Richard Snowden the following Arbitration was recorded April 20, 1759
I Benjamin Welsh, planter of PGCo am held and firmly bound unto Richard Snowden, iron master of Anne Arundel County, Maryland in the sum of 500 pounds sterling this April 7, 1759. The condition of the above obligation is whereas there is a dispute between Benjamin Welsh and Richard Snowden with regard to the beginning tree of a tract called "Rich Neck" and for the deciding and perpetually fixing the beginning the parties have mutually chosen Mr. Joseph Jones, Mr. John Wilmot, Jr., Dr. Joshua Warfield and Capt. Henry Ridgley to be arbitrators and the said Benjamin Welsh shall well and truly stand by and comply with the award and determination of the aforesaid arbitrators. Benjamin Welsh in the presence of Joshua Warfield, John Wilmot, Jr.
Then came Samuel Waters before me and being one of the people called Quakers did solemnly affirm and declare that about 20 years ago there was some company at his father's house and they were discussing controversies arising among

144

the inhabitants of this province in relations to land. My father said he believed that the surveyors were often in fault and by mistake made wrong returns for he said that he had been informed that John Welsh and Thomas Clark had run out William Gray's land and that it ran into Roper's land. He further said he was assured if that was the case that the surveyor had made a return of wrong courses for that he the said father was at the survey when William Gray's land was taken up about 35 or 36 years ago Thomas Clark lodged at my father's house and being in discourse about the lands my father asked him if he had run out Mr. Gray's land and he said Clark answered that he had and it run into Roper's land which was an elder survey. My father answered that if it did the surveyor had made a mistake and made a return of wrong courses. About 17 or 18 years ago my father was called upon to prove the bounds of William Gray's land in about one or two days after the deferment went to the father's house and asked his father if he had found the trees of Gray's land he answered that he had and that he had proved them and Richard Isaac. Also he further said he was at the survey when Gray's land was taken up and they had run from the trees that Richard Isaac and he proved but he said that the land did not run where it did then for that Gray's land was late clear of Roper's land but that the surveyor had made a mistake and ran wrong courses which carried Gray's land into Roper's land which was an elder survey. Samuel Waters

Evidence taken to prove the bounded trees of William Gray's land being two white oak standing in a small draft of the Piney Branch that runs into the Eastern Branch of Potomack River

Mr. Richard Isaac, Sr., aged 80 years declares that 40 years ago or thereabouts old Charles Walker and himself were in these woods and the said Walker told him the two white oaks we are now at for the two bounded trees of William Gray's land and that about 15 or 16 years ago the said Richard Isaac was had before commissioners appointed by court and prove the same trees for Samuel Day to be the bounded trees of William Gray's land and the said Richard Isaac declares that Mr. Robert Tyler was at that time on acquainted with the woods when he took up the land whereon Lewis Duvall now lives and got him to show the said Tyler the woods and further saith not. Richard Isaac, Sr. Mr. Joseph Walker aged 43 years declares that he and his brother Charles Walker were talking some time past about the bounded trees of William Gray's land and he told me of the two bounded white oaks which I took at that time to be the two trees that Mr. Richard Isaac has now proved to be the bounded trees of William Gray's land and that the said Walker told me that one of the trees was either dead or cut down and further saith not. Joseph Walker, August 1, 1758

Mr. Jeremiah Fowler aged 47 years declares that 17 or 18 years ago Mr. Richard Isaac was about line of William Gray's land for him and he came with the said Isaac to run out the land and we began at the same to trees that Mr. Isaac has proved to be the beginning tree's and William Gray's land and running we found it to lie in an older survey and at the same time old Samuel Waters was sent for and after looking about the woods a little came back and to the best of his knowledge prove the same to white oaks to be the bounded trees of William Gray's land and further he saith not Jeremiah Fowler, August 4, 1758

Mr. James Beck age 52 years declares that about 16 or 17 years ago he was a Commissioner for taking evidences to prove the bounds of Gray's land and he was brought to a bounded white oak which he thinks to be the tree that Mr. Isaac has now proved whereon evidences being sworn he thinks Richard Isaac and some others declare that the said white oak was the beginning tree of Gray's land and that they run the same day from the said trees and run into Mr. Henry Wright's plantation and further saith not August 11, 1758 sworn before James Crow, Richard Isaac, Jr.

Whereas Mr. Richard Snowden and Mr. Benjamin Welsh having a dispute about the bounds of a tract of land called Rich Neck taken up by William Gray have entered into bonds bearing date this day in the penalty of 500 pounds sterling to abide by our award and determination we therefore having impartially examine the evidences to us presented by both parties do on consideration of award and determine that the trees insisted on by Mr. Richard Snowden and which have been proved by Mr. Richard Isaac, Sr. and Mr. Samuel Waters, Sr. the beginning trees of the said tract of land called Rich Neck. In witness whereof we have hereunto set our hands and seals this April 7, 1759, Joseph Jones, Joseph Warfield, John Wilmot, Jr., Henry Ridgley

Page 296. At the request of Alexander Symmer the following Deed was recorded April 21, 1759
Indenture made April 4, 1759; Richard Smith, Chyrurgeon of Upper Marlborough Town in consideration of 287 pounds sterling paid by Alexander Symmer, merchant have sold eight lots of land being in Upper Marlborough Town, Lot Number 37, Lot Number 38, Lot Number 39, Lot Number 40, Lot Number 49, Lot Number 50, Lot Number 61 and Lot Number 62 together with all and singular the dwelling houses kitchen staples orchards gardens paling improvements conveniences and advantages. Signed Richard Smith in the presence of John Hepburn, George Clarke and acknowledged before John Hepburn and at the same time Elizabeth Smith wife of Richard Smith relinquished her right of dower

Page 298. At the request of Shadrack Turner the following Deed was recorded May 2, 1759
Indenture made April 9, 1759; Benjamin Belt, Jr. and Andrew Beall, planters in consideration of 35 pounds 10 shillings sterling paid by Shadrack Turner, planter has sold a tract called "Wild Cat" containing 125 acres and beginning at white oak the beginning tree of land formerly in possession of James Leigh called "Friends Goodwill." Signed Benjamin Belt, Jr., Andrew Beall in the presence of and acknowledged before Mordecai Jacob, Thomas Williams and at the same time Ruth Belt wife of Benjamin Belt, Jr. and Margaret Beall wife of Andrew Beall relinquished their right of dower

Page 300. At the request of Josias Talburtt, Basil Talburtt, Thomas Talburtt, Tobias Talburtt, Solomi Talburtt & Thomas Wilcoxon Talburtt the following Bill of Sale was recorded May 2, 1759
I Henry Humphrey for diverse good causes me thereunto

147

moving has given by these presents to Josias Talburtt, Basil Talburtt, Thomas Talburtt, Solomi Talburtt, Tobias Talburtt and Thomas Wilcoxon Talburtt all the Negroes, chattels, household furniture unto each child by a list of the said good and chattels dated April 24, 1759

In witness whereof I have set my hand and seal this May 2, 1759, Henry Humphrey in the presence of John Hepburn, John Graham and acknowledged before John Hepburn

Page 301. At the request of Henry Brookes the following Deed was recorded May 2, 1759

Indenture made May 2, 1759; Mary Craufurd, widow and David Craufurd, merchant in consideration of 7 pounds current money paid by Henry Brookes, Joyner has sold a lot or acre of land in Upper Marlborough Town lying on the west side of the street that leads from the landing up towards the Ball house at the corner of Richard Snowden's lot. Signed Mary Craufurd, David Craufurd in the presence of John Hepburn, Henry King and acknowledged before John Hepburn

Page 303. At the request of Leonard Piles the following Certificate of Stray was recorded May 8, 1759

I certify that Leonard Piles brought before me a large bay colored stray horse, no brand, a small blaze in his face, the off hind foot white. May 8, 1759, J. Sprigg

Page 303. At the request of Richard Snowden the following Bill of Sale was recorded abt May 8, 1759

I Richard Cheney, miner of PGCo in consideration of 54 pounds four shillings and seven pence current money paid by Richard Snowden has sold servant men named William Barbar, John Denis, and Thomas Brooke, Negro Sarah (30 yrs.), Lettis (4 yrs.), Jack (1 yr.), will and horses with all their gear, nine black cattle, 30 hogs and all the rest of my household goods. In witness whereof I have set my hand and seal this April 14, 1759, Richard Cheney in the presence of and acknowledged before Mordecai Jacob

148

Page 304. At the request of Samuel Snowden the following Bill of Sale was recorded abt May 8, 1759

I Samuel Cheney, miner in consideration of 206 pounds three shillings and three pence current money paid by Richard Snowden have sold one white servant man named Robert Barbar, a servant man named William Banks, Negroes Cooke (29 yrs.), Pegg (10 yrs.) and Hannah (7 yrs.), one old stone horse and all and singular my household goods of whatever kind. In witness whereof I have set my hand and seal this April 14, 1759, Samuel Cheney in the presence of and acknowledged before Mordecai Jacob

Page 304. At the request of James Wood the following Certificate of Stray was recorded May 9, 1759

This day Mr. James Wood brought before me a small dark mare taken as up as a stray, branded on the near buttock, has a star and snip and has been lately trimmed. George Gantt

Page 304. At the request of Joseph Sarratt, Jr., the following Certificate of Stray was recorded May 8, 1759

Joseph Sarratt, Jr., brought before me a small dark bay mare taken up as a stray branded on the near shoulder and buttock, has a star and snip in her face and has been lately trimmed. George Gantt

Page 305. At the request of Stephen Watkins the following Deed of Gift was recorded May 12, 1759

I Thomas Harwood, planter in consideration for the love I bear unto my grandson Stephen Watkins of Anne Arundel County, Maryland have given by these presents Negro Moll by virtue of a mortgage of the same to me made by Benjamin Boyd bearing date March 13, 1750 recorded in PGCo. In witness whereof I have hereunto set my hand and affixed my seal this May 4, 1759, Thomas Harwood in the presence of Samuel Smith, Sarah Harwood

Page 305. At the request of Daniel Daily the following Certificate of Stray was recorded May 12, 1759

PGCo, May 11, 1759; this is to certify that Daniel Daily brought before me as a stray a sorrel mare 12 hands 3 inches high with a blaze face, four white feet, branded on the near shoulder and the near thigh. Nathaniel Magruder

Page 305. At the request of Samuel Mason the following Certificate of Stray was recorded May 12, 1759
PGCo, May 7, 1759; this is to certify that Samuel Mason living on Mr. Calvert's Manor brought before me as a stray a small bay horse about 12 ½ hands high, docked and branded on the left thigh, a small star in his forehead and appears to be about four years old. George Gordon

Page 305. At the request of Charles Robinson the following Certificate of Stray was recorded May 12, 1759
PGCo, May 11, 1759; Charles Robinson brought before me a small sorrel horse about 11 hands high, has a blaze in his face, no brand that is visible and he complains he is troublesome and breaks into his inclosures. Christopher Lowndes

Page 305. At the request of William Mason the following Certificate of Stray was recorded May 15, 1759
William Mason brought before me a stray a black mare about 12 ½ hands high with a small star in her forehead, no perceivable brand. May 12, 1759, Nathaniel Magruder

Page 305. At the request of Lewis Mollohon the following Certificate of Stray was recorded May 16, 1759
PGCo, May 14, 1759; Lewis Mollohon brought before me a small black stallion about 12 hands high, neither branded nor docked and seems to be about four years old, he complains he is troublesome and breaks into his inclosures. Signed Christopher Lowndes

Page 306. At the request of George Cross the following Certificate of Stray was recorded May 19, 1759
PGCo, May 16, 1759; George Cross brought before me as a trespasser and stray a small sorrel mare, a blaze in her face,

branded on the near buttock. Mordecai Jacob

Page 306. At the request of Benjamin Whales [sic Wailes] the following Certificate of Stray was recorded May 21, 1759
PGCo, May 17, 1759; Benjamin Whales brought before me a small dark bay horse branded on the near buttock and shoulder, has three white feet, a star in his forehead. George Gantt

Page 306. At the request of James Lucas the following Certificate of Stray was recorded May 30, 1759
PGCo, May 23, 1759; James Lucas who lives on the Western Branch of Patuxent this day brought before me taken up as a stray a black mare that is neither docked nor branded, she is about 12 hands high and has a colt 3 weeks old, and she appears to be 4 years old. John Cooke

Page 306. At the request of James Gibbs the following Certificate of Stray was recorded May 30, 1759
PGCo, May 30, 1759; this certifies that James Gibbs, Sr., by his son William Gibbs brought before me as a stray a black horse about 13 hands high and seven or eight years old, docked and branded on the off thigh, a star in his forehead. George Gordon

Page 306. At the request of Robert Wade, 3rd the following Certificate of Stray was recorded May 30, 1759
PGCo, May 26, 1759; this certifies that Robert Wade, 3rd brought before me as a stray a small sorrel mare about 12 hands high, 4 years old docked and branded on the near buttock. George Gordon

Page 306. At the request of Thomas Waring the following Deed was recorded June 2, 1759
Indenture made June 2, 1759; Charles Boteler, planter in consideration of 5 shillings current money paid by Thomas Waring, Gentleman doth by these presents sell and assigned forever all the remaining part of a tract called "Beall's Pleasure" containing 250 acres lying on the Beaver Dam Branch of Potomack River where Benjamin Warrenford land leaves off.

Signed Charles Boteler in the presence of and acknowledged before John Cooke, Nathaniel Magruder and at the same time Sophia Boteler wife of Charles Boteler relinquished her right of dower

Page 307. At the request of James Pelly the following Certificate of Stray was recorded June 2, 1759
I hereby certify that James Pelley brought before me as a stray a small white mare, branded not known appears to be very old and poor given under my hand this June 2, 1759, J. Sprigg

Page 307. At the request of Thomas Hilleary the following Certificate of Stray was recorded June 9, 1759
This day Mr. Thomas Hilleary brought before me as a trespasser and stray a small gray mare branded on the near shoulder and near thigh, shod before and had a switch tail. Thomas Williams

Page 307. At the request of Samuel Hanson the following Assignment of a Mortgage was recorded June 11, 1759
Charles County, Maryland, I hereby assign all my right title and claim into a mortgage made to me by Leonard Marbury and recorded among the records of Prince George's County [Vide Mortgage Folio 107] to Samuel Hanson and my title and interest to the several Negroes mentioned in the said mortgage for value received of the said Hanson. As witness my hand and seal this May 25, 1759, Thomas Marshall in the presence of James Smallwood, Jr.

Page 308. At the request of Hugh Wilson the following Certificate of Stray was recorded June 9, 1759
PGCo, June 5, 1759; Hugh Wilson brought before me a chestnut sorrel horse about 13 hands high, no visible brand and complains he is troublesome and breaks into his inclosures. Christopher Lowndes

Page 308. At the request of James Buckman the following Certificate of Stray was recorded June 9, 1759
PGCo, June 5, 1759; James Buckman brought before me a bright

sorrel mare about 14 hands high, branded on the near buttock with the letter I, some white saddle spots and a blaze in her face he complains she is troublesome and breaks into his inclosures. Christopher Lowndes

Page 308. At the request of James Gibbs the following Certificate of Stray was recorded June 12, 1759
PGCo, June 5, 1759; taken up as a stray and brought before me by James Gibbs a small bay horse branded on the left buttock and a star in his forehead. George Gantt.

Page 308. At the request of John Tolson the following Deed was recorded June 13, 1759
Indenture made May 31, 1759; John Abington and Andrew Abington, Gentlemen and Mrs. Mary Scott their mother in consideration of 395 pounds currency paid by John Tolson, planter has sold tracts called "Speedwell" being John Abington's dwelling plantation containing 138 acres; Irving containing 150 acres; and 91 acres being part of part "Goodwill" (containing 191 acres in the whole). Signed John Abington, Andrew Abington, Mary Scott in the presence of John Watson, George Parker and acknowledged before Nathaniel Magruder, George Gordon

Page 310. At the request of Edward Burch the following Deed was recorded June 9, 1759
Indenture made May 28, 1759; Ann Davis and her son Ephraim Davis, planters of Frederick County, Maryland in consideration of 22 pounds current money paid by Edward Burch of PGCo as also for good causes and considerations there unto moving has sold part of a tract called "Weavers Prospect" containing 100 acres lying near the Eastern Branch and bounded by "The Ridge." Signed Ann Davis, Ephraim Davis in the presence of John Darnall, Henry Darnall, Jr., and acknowledged before John Darnall

Page 310. At the request of Enoch Jenkins the following Deed was recorded May 31, 1759

We Daniel Jenkins and Ruth Jenkins in consideration of the natural affection we have and do bear to our beloved son Enoch Jenkins, planter as also for divers other good causes and considerations me hereunto moving do give by these presents during his natural life part of a tract called "Port Royal" containing 50 acres. In witness whereof we have hereunto set our hands and seals this May 31, 1759, Daniel Jenkins, Ruth Jenkins in the presence of and acknowledged before George Gordon, Nathaniel Magruder and at the same time Ruth Jenkins wife of Daniel Jenkins relinquished her right of dower
{Port Royal originally patented to John Peirce, Sep 23, 1685, Charles County Liber 22 f 267}

Page 311. At the request of Thomas Snowden the following Certificate of Stray was recorded June 13, 1759
I hereby certify that Mr. Thomas Snowden has brought before me as a stray a middle sized bay mare branded on the near shoulder and buttock's and off shoulder, has a star in her forehead and the owner not being known Mr. Snowden is hereby empowered to use the aforesaid mare. June 2, 1759, John Contee

Page 311. At the request of William Digges the following Certificate of Stray was recorded June 13, 1759
PGCo Sct, June 11, 1759; this certifies that Mr. William Digges, Potomack, sent before me by William Dorch his overseer, a stray black horse about 14 hands high, his two hind feet white, a blaze in his face down to his nose, docked and branded on the off thigh. George Gordon

Page 311. At the request of Isaac Brashear the following Certificate of Stray was recorded June 19, 1759
PGCo Sct, June 14, 1759; Isaac Brashear brought before me as a trespasser and stray a small bay horse branded on the off thigh, has a small star in his forehead. Thomas Williams

Page 311. At the request of Susanna Magruder the following Deed was recorded June 16, 1759

Indenture made December 20, 1758; James Willett, planter in consideration of 80 pounds current money paid by Susanna Magruder has sold part of a tract called "Buttington" containing 62 acres and bounded by "Good Luck". Signed James Willett in the presence of and acknowledged before George Gordon, Nathaniel Magruder and at the same time Amy Willett wife of James Willett relinquished her right of dower {Susanna Bussey widow of Alexander Magruder. The tract "Butlinton" was patented by Henry Truman for 462 Acres in 1737, MSA S1596-0904}

Page 313. At the request of John Rushbrooks the following Marks of hogs & Cattle was recorded June 22, 1759; a crop and a slit in the left ear, a slit and under bit in the right ear

Page 313. At the request of George Bean the following Land Commission was recorded abt June 22, 1759
Memorandum that on the special petition of George Bean preferred to the justices of Prince George's County, Maryland on the 4th Tuesday in November in the 8th year of his Lordship commission the Right Hon. the Lord Proprietary Dominion etc., his Lordship commission issued by order of the justices aforesaid out of the county aforesaid on the 15th day of January Anno Domini 1759. In these words following, Frederick Absolute Lord and Proprietary of the Province of Maryland and Avalon Lord Baron of Baltimore vizt; to Messrs Andrew Hamilton, James Tannehill, Charles Beall and Walter Evans of PGCo Gentleman, whereas George Bean, is seized of a tract called "The Ridge" and preferred his petition in writing to our county court held at Upper Marlborough Town before Joseph Belt Jr., Gentleman and his associates then and still justices within our county to examine evidence to prove and perpetuate the memory of the bounds of the said tract of land. Therefore, we command you any three or two of you to examine all witnesses or persons concerned touching their knowledge of the bounds of the said tract. Witness Joseph Belt, Jr., Gentleman, June 30, 1758. Issued January 15, 1759, Joseph Sim, Clk
In pursuant to a commission to examine evidences to prove the

bounds of "The Ridge" lying at the mouth of the Eastern Branch of Potomack River on the east side we hereby give notice that we intend to meet at the lands on Saturday, April 14th next. Witness our hands and seals this March 17, 1759

William Masters aged 70 years or thereabouts being at a place where there is now a stone fixed marked '1759 GB' where a white oak stump then stood and southward of a place known by the name of The Pons deposes that about 30 years ago he was at the boundary of two trees a white oak and a black oak and the white oak stump above described was one of them and that was bounded by Richard Weaver for the beginning of a tract called "The Ridge"

Benjamin Talbott aged 49 declares about 27 years ago Lewis Wilcoxon showed him the white oak as described before and told him it was the beginning tree of a tract called "The Ridge" and that he marked a red oak for fear the white oak by fire or some other accident should be destroyed.

Thomas Garton, aged 57 or thereabouts, saith that about 20 years ago Lewis Wilcoxon and John Carr came to erect a school house and they agreed with John Carr to cut down the timber for school house and the two trees mentioned he believes were cut down and were the bounded trees of "The Ridge".

Given under our hands and seals, Walter Evans, Andrew Hamilton, James Tannehill

Page 314. At the request of Mareen Duvall the following Land Commission was recorded abt June 22, 1759

Memorandum that on the special petition of Mareen Duvall preferred to the justices of Prince George's County, Maryland on the 4th Tuesday in June in the 8th year of his Lordship commission the Right Hon. the Lord Proprietary Dominion etc., his Lordship commission issued by order of the justices aforesaid out of the county aforesaid on the 10th day of July Anno Domini 1758. In these words following, Frederick Absolute Lord and Proprietary of the Province of Maryland and Avalon Lord Baron of Baltimore vizt; to Messrs Samuel Magruder, James Magruder Jr., Zadock Magruder and Jeremiah Berry of PGCo Gentleman, whereas Mareen Duvall, is seized of

part of a tract called "Vale of Benjamin" called "Copton Hills" and preferred his petition in writing to our county court held at Upper Marlborough Town before Joseph Belt, Jr., Gentleman and his associates then and still justices within our county to examine evidence to prove and perpetuate the memory of the bounds of the said tract of land. Therefore, we command you any three or two of you to examine all witnesses or persons concerned touching their knowledge of the bounds of the said tract. Witness Joseph Belt, Jr., Gentleman, June 30, 1758. Issued July 10, 1758, Joseph Sim, Clk
Pages 315 is missing

Page 316.　At the request of John Lanham the following Supersedes was recorded June 26, 1759
You John Lanham, William Lanham and Thomas Morris do confess judgment to Mr. Turner Wootton for 233-1/2 pounds of tobacco and 2 shillings currency which sums were recovered on June 21, 1759 before me one of His Lordships Justices of the Peace to be levied on your goods chattels lands or tenements for the use of Turner Wootton in case John Lanham shall not pay and satisfy the said sum and costs thereon on February 10th next. Witness my hand June 21, 1759, George Gordon

Page 316.　At the request of William Mason the following Supersedes was recorded June 26, 1759
You William Mason, Thomas Morris and William Lanham do confess judgment to Mr. Turner Wootton for 30 pounds of tobacco and one shilling current money which sums were recovered on May 18, 1759 before me one of His Lordships Justices of the Peace to be levied on your goods chattels lands or tenements for the use of Turnor Wootton in case William Mason shall not pay and satisfy the said sum and costs thereon on February 10th next. Witness my hand this June 21, 1759, George Gordon

Page 316.　At the request of Benjamin Moore the following Supersedes was recorded June 26, 1759
You Benjamin Moore, James Burgess and Francis Hudson do

confess judgment to Mr. Turner Wootton for 255 pounds of tobacco and two shillings current money which sums were recovered on June 20, 1759 before me one of His Lordships Justices of the Peace to be levied on your goods chattels lands or tenements for the use of Turnor Wootton in case Benjamin Moore shall not pay and satisfy the said sum and costs thereon on February 10th next. Witness my hand this June 22, 1759, George Gordon

Page 316. At the request of Eleazer Lanham the following Certificate of Stray was recorded June 26, 1759
PGCo Sct, June 22, 1759; this certifies that Eleazer Lanham brought before me as a stray a small sorrel mare about three years old and 11 ½ hands high, docked and branded on the near thigh. George Gordon

Page 316. At the request of Thomas Shearwood the following Deed was recorded June 27, 1759
Indenture made June 27, 1759; William Piles in consideration of 1200 pounds currency paid by Thomas Shearwood has sold part of a tract called "Hunters Field" containing 60 acres. Signed William Piles in the presence of John Hepburn, John Tolson and acknowledged before John Hepburn

Page 317. At the request of John Orme the following Deed was recorded June 27, 1759
Indenture made March 9, 1759; Thomas Pratt, planter in consideration of 100 pounds sterling money of Great Britain paid by John Orme, carpenter and son of the Rev. John Orme, deceased has sold part of a tract called "The Lucky Discovery" containing 119 ¼ acres lying on the west side of the Western Branch of Patuxent River beginning at the end of the second line of a tract called "The Free School Farm" now in possession of Ignatius Digges, Esq., signed Thomas Pratt in the presence of and acknowledged before Mordecai Jacob, Thomas Williams and at the same time Eleanor Pratt wife of Thomas Pratt relinquished her right of dower

Page 319. At the request of John Tolson the following Deed was recorded June 27, 1759
Indenture made June 27, 1759; William Piles, planter in consideration of 8 pounds 15 shillings paid by John Tolson and for other good considerations him thereunto moving has sold part of a tract called "Hunters Folly" containing 42 acres and beginning at a bounded black oak standing on the south side of the ridge main road as leads from Broad Creek to Upper Marlborough Town; and also 26 acres being part of "Hunters Field" being all the remaining part which is in the possession of William Piles excepting 1 acre reserved for burying ground. Signed William Piles, in the presence of John Hepburn, Thomas Shearwood and acknowledged before John Hepburn

Page 321. At the request of Robert Wall the following Deed of Gift was recorded June 27, 1759
I George Naylor, planter attorney for Thomas Wall of Dorsett [sic Dorchester], County, Maryland for executing this deed of gift as by his power of attorney to me dated June 19, 1759 more fully appear send greeting know ye that I the said George Naylor for divers causes and valuable considerations me hereunto moving have given by these presents unto Robert Wall, planter all that part of a tract called "Ward's Pasture" containing 60 acres beginning at a bounded popular standing on the main north branch of Deep Creek. Signed George Naylor in the presence of John Hepburn, Thomas Wall and acknowledged before John Hepburn

Page 321. At the request of Robert Peter the following Mortgage was recorded June 27, 1759
Indenture made June 5, 1759; between Barton Lucas of PGCo and Robert Peter merchant of Frederick County, Maryland. Witnessed that whereas Barton Lucas does owe and stand indebted to John Glassford and Company the sum of 50 pounds current money of Maryland which Robert Peter at the special instance and request of Barton Lucas has paid and satisfied and discharged in consideration thereof and also the sum of five shillings current money has sold by these presents all that part

of the tract called "Hop Yard" which was willed to the said Barton Lucas by Thomas Lucas, deceased. Provided nevertheless that if Barton Lucas shall well and truly pay and satisfy unto Robert Peter the aforesaid sum of money with legal interest to commence on the first day of June 1760 or before the first day of June 1762 then this deed shall be void. Signed Barton Lucas in the presence of Ebenezer Fisher, John Darnall and acknowledged before [page 323 missing]

Page 324.   At the request of John Mahue the following Supersedes was recorded June 27, 1759
You John Mahue, James Mahue and William Nelson do confess judgment to James Wardrop for the sum of 2 pound 8 shillings and 2 pence current money of Maryland which sums were recovered on June 16, 1759 before me one of His Lordships Justices of the Peace to be levied on your goods chattels lands or tenements for the use of James Wardrop in case John Mahue shall not pay and satisfy the said sum and costs thereon on February 10th next. Thomas Williams

Page 324.   At the request of Thomas Webb, Jr. the following Certificate of Stray was recorded June 27, 1759
PGCo Sct, June 25, 1759; I certify that Thomas Webb, Jr., brought before me as a trespasser and stray a small black mare branded on the near thigh, has a small star in her forehead. Thomas Williams

Page 324.   At the request of John Brashear the following Supersedes was recorded June 28, 1759
You John Brashear, Sr., Thomas Brashear and Benjamin Brashear do confess judgment to Sarah Lamar, executrix of John Lamar, Jr., deceased for the sum of 6 pound 13 shillings and 6 pence sterling and 311-1/4 pounds of tobacco and is which sums were recovered on the fourth Tuesday of March to be levied on your goods chattels lands or tenements for the use of Sarah Lamar in case John Brashear, Sr., shall not pay and satisfy the said sum and costs thereon on February 10th next. Taken and acknowledged this May 25th 1759 before us Mordecai Jacob,

160

Robert Tyler

Page 324. At the request of Isaac Brashear the following Supersedes was recorded June 28, 1759
You Isaac Brashear, John Brashear, Sr. and John Brashear, Jr. do confess judgment to Sarah Lamar, executrix of John Lamar, Jr., deceased for the sum of 4 pounds seven shillings three pence half penny debt and 236 ½ pounds of tobacco and six pence currency costs which sums were recovered on the fourth Tuesday in March to be levied on your goods chattels lands or tenements for the use of Sarah Lamar in case Isaac Brashear shall not pay and satisfy the said sum and costs thereon on February 10th next. Taken and acknowledged this May 25th 1759 before us Mordecai Jacob, Robert Tyler

Page 324. At the request of John Gibson the following Supersedes was recorded June 28, 1759
You John Gibson, Benjamin Berry, Jr. and Henry Brookes do confess judgment to Turnor Wootton, Esq. for the sums of 31 pounds 15 shillings and two pence current money and 30 shillings and 10 pence sterling money and also 300-1/4 pounds weight of tobacco which sums were recovered on the fourth Tuesday of March last to be levied on your goods chattels lands or tenements for the use of Peregrine Mackaness in case John Gibson shall not pay and satisfy the said sum and costs thereon on February 10th next. Taken and acknowledged before me June 26, 1759, John Hepburn

Page 325. At the request of Zachariah Bond the following Deed was recorded June 28, 1759
Indenture made March 23, 1759; Thomas Dyar by virtue of the award of Messrs. Thomas Marshall, Bayne Smallwood and John Stoddert of Charles County, Maryland Gentleman arbitrators indifferently elected and chosen between Thomas Dyar and William Hicks of St. Mary's County, Maryland being now possessed in his right of 100 acres of land lying in Prince George's County being part of a tract formerly granted unto William Calvert, Esq. for 3000 acres commonly called and

known by the name of Piscattaway Manor otherwise "Calvert's Manor" (alias Elizabeth Manor) lying in a part of the manor formerly in possession of Thomas Edelen for 400 acres and bounded as follows; beginning at a Locust post and a ashen swamp near Potomack River the reputed beginning of the said Manor and bounded by the Accokeek Branch, the 600 acres in possession of Thomas Noble. Now this indenture further witness that Thomas Dyar in consideration of 63 guineas paid by Zachariah Bond has sold the aforesaid 100 acres of land being part of 400 acres formerly in possession of Thomas Edelen. Signed Thomas Dyar in the presence of Joseph Beall, Jr., Henry Greenfield Sothoron and acknowledged before Nathaniel Magruder, George Gordon and at the same time Henrietta Dyar wife of Thomas Dyar relinquished her right of dower

Page 326. At the request of Samuel Bussey & Thomas Harvey the following Mortgage was recorded June 28, 1759
I Timothy Drew, blacksmith in consideration of 28 pounds 14 shillings and 4 pence sterling money of England paid by Samuel Bussey and Thomas Harvey, planters have sold Negroes Nan and Nell. Provided nevertheless that if Timothy Drew shall well and truly pay unto Samuel Bussey and Thomas Harvey the aforesaid sum of money with interest at any time then this Bill of Sale to be void. Given under my hand and seal this June 20, 1759, Timothy Drew in the presence of and acknowledged before Nathaniel Magruder

Page 327. At the request of John Dorsett the following Deed was recorded July 3, 1759
Indenture made June 26, 1759; Robert Wall, planter in consideration of 40 pounds currency money paid by John Dorsett, planter has sold a tract containing 220 acres within the following courses; beginning at the intersection of "Smith's Pasture" to "Stoake" to the first bound tree. Signed Robert Wall, in the presence of John Hepburn, George Naylor and acknowledged before John Hepburn
{"Stoke" and "Stoake" is used interchangeably in PGCo land records for this tract. Murphy Ward d. 1709 first patented

162

"Stoke" in 1689 and in his will gave 70 acres of "Stoake" to Thomas Wall. Later, "Stoke" was taken up and included in the bounds of "Woodbridge."}

Page 328. At the request of Enoch Magruder the following Mortgage was recorded June 28, 1759
I Abraham Russell, planter in consideration of 2210 pounds crop tobacco paid by Enoch Magruder have sold by these presents 1 feather bed and furniture, 2 iron pots, 1 trading gun, 2 sorrel mares, 1 cow and calf, 1 brindle cow, one yearling, 9 hogs. Provided that if Abraham Russell shall well and truly pay unto Enoch Magruder the aforesaid tobacco at or upon the 10th day of June next with legal interest at the Queen Ann Warehouse then this indenture to be void. In witness whereof I have hereunto set my hand and seal this June 26, 1759, Abraham Russell in the presence of and acknowledged before Thomas Williams

Page 329. At the request of John Tolson the following Release was recorded July 13, 1759
I James Marshall, merchant in consideration of 350 pounds current money of Maryland paid by John Tolson, Gentleman have released and quit claimed all too 3 tracts called "Goodwill" containing 190 acres, "Speedwell" containing 138 acres and "Irvine" containing 150 acres which were mortgaged to me by John Abington. In witness whereof I have hereunto set my hand and seal this July 7, 1759, James Marshall in the presence of John Hepburn, Thomas Somes and acknowledged before John Hepburn

Page 329. At the request of Locklen McIntosh the following Certificate of Stray was recorded July 11, 1759
PGCo Sct, July 11, 1759; this certifies that Locklen McIntosh brought before me as a stray a grey mare, docked and branded on the near thigh, 10 or 12 years old and has been troublesome to him and the neighbors the 6 or 7 years past. She now has 2 mare colts the one 2 year old and the other 1-year-old both of the deep bay color. July 10, 1759, George Gordon

Page 330. At the request of John Contee the following Deed was recorded July 15, 1759
Indenture made July 12, 1759; Thomas Lucas Carpenter of Baltimore County, Maryland in consideration of 100 pounds sterling paid by John Contee of PGCo as also for diverse good causes and considerations him thereunto moving has sold a tract called "Largo" containing 250 acres. Signed Thomas Lucas in the presence of John Hepburn, George Gordon and acknowledged before John Hepburn

Page 331. At the request of Sarah Robison the following Certificate of Stray was recorded July 18, 1759
PGCo Sct, July 14, 1759; Sarah Robison brought before me a middle size bay horse taken up as a stray, branded on the left shoulder has a star in his forehead. George Gantt

Page 331. At the request of Francis Piles the following Lease was recorded July 19, 1759
Indenture made July 18, 1759; William Piles, planter in consideration of the rents and covenants to be performed and for other causes and considerations him thereunto moving has demised and to farm let unto Francis Piles that part of a tract called "Hunters Folly" containing 75 acres and beginning at a bound box oak on that part of the land which William Mason now dwells. To have and to hold from the date of these presents for the term of 99 years paying yearly the sum of 4 shillings sterling at or upon July 10th yearly. Signed William Piles in the presence of John Hepburn, John Panner and acknowledged before John Hepburn

Page 332. At the request of Thomas Clark the following Deed was recorded July 15, 1759
Indenture made July 2, 1759; Basil Waring, Gentleman in consideration of 13 pistoles paid by Thomas Clark, Esqr., has sold part of a tract called "St. Andrews" which was formerly the dwelling plantation of William Powell which Basil Waring lately purchased of Fielder Powell and Osborn Powell containing 34 ½ acres and also that part piece being part of St. Andrews which

164

Basil Waring lately purchased of John Hallam containing 10 acres and in the whole 44 ½ acres. Signed Basil Waring in the presence of and acknowledged before John Cooke, Thomas Williams and at the same time Susannah Waring wife of Basil Waring relinquished her right of dower

Page 334. At the request of Thomas Gantt the following Deed was recorded April 7, 1759
Indenture made October 19, 1758; Josias Beall, Jr., Gentleman in consideration of 278 pounds sterling paid by Thomas Gantt, 3rd, Gentleman has sold part of two tracts of land called "Fathers Gift" and "Beall's Adventure" alias "Good Luck" containing 371 acres and bounded by Cabin Branch, Pottinger's land, and the dividing line of Lowndes part of "Good Luck" taken up and so called by Wade and Gardiner. Signed Josias Beall, Jr. in the presence of and acknowledged before George Gantt, Nathaniel Magruder

Page 335. At the request of John Ryon & James Ryon the following Bill of Sale was recorded July 21, 1759
I Nathaniel Ryon, planter in consideration of the diverse sums of money and tobacco due from me unto Hancock Lee and also unto Mr. Stephen West, merchants which sums are secured by John Ryon and James Ryon, planters have sold by these presents unto John Ryon and James Ryon 2 cows and 1 calf, 1 heifer 1 black mare 1 mouse colored colt and 1 feather bed and furniture.
In witness whereof I have set my hand and seal this July 10, 1759, Nathaniel Ryon in the presence of Peter Robinson, John Healy and acknowledged before John Hepburn

Page 336. At the request of Thomas Drane the following Deed was recorded July 21, 1759
Indenture made March 16, 1694; Francis Swanson of Calvert County, Maryland, planter in consideration of 6000 pounds of good merchantable leaf tobacco and cask paid by Thomas Plummer of Calvert County, Maryland, planter has sold part of a tract called "Swanson's Lot" containing 150 acres lying in

Calvert County, Maryland on the west side of the northern branch of Patuxent River in the woods and beginning at Bowes Brooke. Signed Francis Swanson, Susanna Swanson in the presence of Thomas Davis, Thomas Stafford

On the back of the deed was thus endorsed

Memorandum that the lands and premises within mentioned was before us two of the Justices of the Peace for you County of Calvert and acknowledged by Francis Swanson to be the right of Thomas Plummer forever acknowledged and at the same time Susanna Swanson wife of Francis Swanson relinquished her right of dower. In testimony whereof we have hereunto subscribed our names this 6th day of March 1694 Thomas Greenfield, William Barton, Sr.

Page 338. At the request of William Ranter the following Certificate of Stray was recorded July 24, 1759

PGCo Sct; July 23, 1759; William Ranter brought before me a small black mare taken up as a stray has a star in her forehead her right hind foot white, branded on the left shoulder in the left buttock. George Gantt

Page 338. At the request of Samuel Lewis the following Certificate of Stray was recorded July 25, 1759

Samuel Lewis brought before me two horses, one a bay about 12 hands high with a switch tail branded on the off buttock, trots and gallops; the other a dark bay about 13 hands high branded on the off buttock, trots and gallops has a switch tail and complains they are troublesome and breaks into his enclosures. Given under my hand this July 21, 1759 Christopher Lowndes

Page 338. At the request of Gerard Truman Greenfield the following Certificate of Stray was recorded July 25, 1759

PGCo Sct; July 23, 1759; Mr. Gerard Truman Greenfield brought before me a small dark bay horse taken up as a stray, branded on the right buttock. George Gantt

Page 338. At the request of John Brown, brazier the following

166

Supersedes was recorded July 28, 1759
You John Brown, brazier, William Wilcoxon and John Ridgeway do confess judgment to John Ouchterlony for the sum of 66 pounds of tobacco which sum was recovered on July 21, 1759 before me one of His Lordships Justices of the Peace to be levied on your goods chattels lands or tenements for the use of John Ouchterlony in case John Brown, brazier shall not pay and satisfy the said sum and costs thereon on February 10th next. Acknowledged before me the subscriber July 28, 1759, John Contee

Page 338. At the request of Lancelot Wilson the following Certificate of Stray was recorded August 3, 1759
PGCo Sct; August 2, 1759; I hereby certify that Lancelot Wilson brought before me as a stray a very small grey stone horse with a white face, not more than 12 hands high, branded on the near shoulder and buttock appears about 4 years old, has been rode, trots and gallops, hanging mane and switch tail. John Cooke

Page 338. At the request of William Digges the following Certificate of Stray was recorded August 3, 1759
PGCo Sct; July 30, 1759; Mr. William Digges William Digges brought before me a light bay horse about 12 hands high branded on the near buttock, complains he is troublesome and breaks into his enclosures. Christopher Lowndes

Page 338. At the request of Dr. Thomas Hamilton the following Deed was recorded August 7, 1759
Indenture made July 13, 1759; John Orme and James Harvey in consideration of 5 shillings sterling paid by Dr. Thomas Hamilton has sold part of a tract called Calvert's Manor containing 60 acres now in the possession and adjoining to the dwelling plantation of Dr. Thomas Hamilton. Signed John Orme, James Harvey in the presence of John Hepburn, Thomas Brooke and acknowledged before John Hepburn and at the same time Eleanor Harvey wife of James Harvey relinquished her right of dower

Page 340. At the request of Thomas Pratt & Samuel Turner the following Bill of Sale was recorded August 14, 1759
I Richard Beall, planter in consideration of the sums of 2632 ¼ pounds of tobacco and 1 pound 10 shillings and 3 pence current money have sold unto Thomas Pratt and Samuel Turner Negro girl Henny, 1 bay mare, 1 black mare, 3 cows and calves. Provided nevertheless that if Richard Beall shall well and truly pay unto Thomas Pratt and Samuel Turner the aforesaid sums of money and tobacco on or before June 1, 1760 for the redemption of the said bargained premises then this writing or Bill of Sale to be void. In witness whereof I have set my hand and seal this August 7, 1759, Richard Beall in the presence of Mordecai Jacob, Jemima Jacob and acknowledged before Mordecai Jacob

Page 340. At the request of Thomas Cramphin the following Bill of Sale was recorded August 14, 1759
I Adam Miller in consideration of 21 pounds 4 shillings and 5 pence paper money of Maryland paid by Thomas Cramphin have sold Negro woman named Hannah (32 yrs.). Provided nevertheless that if Adam Miller shall well and truly pay unto Thomas Cramphin the aforesaid sum of money on the 28th day of May 1761 then this writing and Bill of Sale to be void. In witness whereof I have set my hand and seal this July 26, 1759, Adam Miller in the presence of and acknowledged before Christopher Lowndes

Page 341. At the request of Rachel Clifford, Mary Docke Lee & Alice Sinclair the following Bill of Sale was recorded August 15, 1759
I John Clifford planter in consideration of 15 pounds current money of Maryland paid by Rachel Clifford, Mary Docke Lee and Alice Sinclair have sold 1 brindle cow, 2 brindle heifer's 17 hogs, 1 black horse 1 small mare, 1 feather bed and furniture, 1 bay mare with a bald face, 4 cider casks containing about hundred gallons each. In witness whereof I have set my hand and seal this August 11, 1759, John Clifford in the presence of Peter Robinson, John Healy and acknowledged before John Hepburn

Page 342. At the request of Edward Perry the following Certificate of Stray was recorded August 18, 1759
PGCo Sct; August 10, 1759; I hereby certify that Edward Perry brought before me a small gray mouse colored mare, 3 years old, docked and branded. J. Sprigg

Page 342. At the request of George Conn, Jr. the following Certificate of Stray was recorded August 28, 1759
George Conn, Jr., brought before me a black stallion about 13 hands high, branded on the near shoulder, paces naturally he complains that he is troublesome and breaks into his enclosures. Given under my hand this August 27, 1759, Christopher Lowndes

Page 343. At the request of Samuel Waters the following Certificate of Stray was recorded July 14, 1759
PGCo Sct; July 11, 1759; Mr. Samuel Waters brought before me as a trespasser and stray a small black mare, no perceivable brand, some saddle spots on her back. Mordecai Jacob

Page 343. At the request of Daniel Frasier of Broad Creek the following Certificate of Stray was recorded August 28, 1759
PGCo Sct; August 25, 1759; Daniel Frasier of Broad Creek brought before me as a stray a black horse, docked and branded on the near shoulder and thigh, some saddle spots, about 13 hands high and 12 to 13 years old. George Gordon

INDEX

William, 21, 27, 77, 78
Beans
Thomas, 22
Beaven
Charles, 34, 36, 37, 38, 95, 96
Beck
James, 61, 62, 146
James, Jr., 87, 106
Beckett
Benjamin, 30
Becraft
Benjamin, 37, 38
Belt
Benjamin, Jr., 96, 97, 124, 147
Jeremiah, Jr., 44, 45, 109, 111, 112, 113
John, Jr., 16
Joseph, 3, 20, 23, 24, 28, 30, 31, 32, 60, 66, 100, 110, 114, 119, 132
Joseph, 3rd, 78
Joseph, Jr., 85, 87
Joseph, Jr. (JP), 3, 20, 24, 28, 31, 32, 47, 60, 62, 66, 69, 87, 100, 107, 108, 109, 111, 112, 114, 117, 118, 119, 123, 127, 130, 132, 133, 134, 135, 136, 137, 138, 141, 155, 157
Margery, 23, 24, 30, 31
Ruth, 96, 97, 147
Tobias, 122
Berry
Benjamin, 27, 85, 94, 101, 126, 128, 139

Benjamin, Jr., 78, 126, 161
Benjamin, Sr., 101
Jeremiah, 101, 131, 156
John, 105
Biggs
George, 7, 8, 9, 10, 135
Samuel, 56, 57
Biscoe
Basil, 55, 56, 74, 75, 91, 98
James (JP), 55, 56, 74, 75, 91, 98
Blacklock
Charity, 79
Thomas, 79, 80, 81
Bladen
Thomas, 103
Blanford
Thomas, 92, 93
Boarman
Joseph, 97, 98, 125, 126
Richard B., 73
Bolton
Bartholomew, 5
Bond
Zachariah, 161, 162
Boteler
Charles, 25, 151, 152
Charles, Sr., 134
Edward, 134
Henry, 48
Sophia, 152
Thomas, 48
Bowdon
George, 70, 71
Bowie
Allen, 123
William, 22, 46, 64, 107, 108

Bowles
  John, 93
Bowling
  John, 125
Bowman
  Thomas, 66
Box
  Thomas, 141
Boyd
  Benjamin, 149
  Thomas, 44, 106
Braddock
  Henry, 5
Bradford
  John, 118, 119
Bradley
  Robert, 33, 34, 35, 36, 37,
    38, 108, 126
Brashear
  Benjamin, 87, 96, 160
  Benjamin, Sr., 133
  Ignatius, 96
  Isaac, 47, 95, 154, 161
  Jeremiah, 101
  John, 17, 47, 87, 88, 106,
    160, 161
  John s/o John, 17
  John, Jr., 161
  John, Sr., 17, 47, 86, 87,
    160
  Mary, 88
  Samuel, 133
  Thomas, 88, 160
  Thomas, Jr., 88
  William, 99
  William, Sr., 133
Brewster
  Thomas (Brouster), 128

Brice
  John, 120
Bright
  William, 14, 15
Brightwell
  Ann, 5
  John, 3, 72, 73
  John, Jr., 5
  Thomas, 3
Brooke
  Benjamin, 38, 137, 138
  Clement, 36
  Isaac, 128, 131
  James, 34, 92, 108
  Jane, 38
  John, 108
  Leonard, 12
  Richard, 128, 131
  Thomas, 63, 64, 96, 131,
    137, 138, 140, 148, 167
  Thomas, Jr., 131, 137
Brookes
  Benjamin, 24, 25, 124
  Henry, 148, 161
Brown
  John, 106, 133, 166, 167
  Peter, 58
  W., 84
  William, 69
Buckman
  James, 70, 152
Bullman
  John, 76, 102
Burch
  Edward, 2, 3, 153
  Francis, 41
  John, 41
  Jonathan, 39

Burgess
  Basil, 132
Burnes
  David, 144
  James, 78
Burns
  James, 11, 144
Bussey
  Samuel, 162
  Susanna, 155
Butleblunt
  James, 54
Butt
  Edward, 6
  Thomas, 6
Calvert
  Benedict, 33, 57
  William, 55, 74, 75, 91, 97,
    98, 125, 126, 161
Campbell
  John, 93
Canaday
  Cornelius, 94
Carnes
  Margaret, 83
Carnole
  Samuel, 51
Carr
  John, 156
Carrick
  John, 76, 102
Carroll
  Charles, 86, 96, 120
  Charles, Jr., 53, 86, 88, 89
  Daniel, 53
  Eleanor, 53
  Elizabeth, 96

Casteel
  Edmund, 4, 79, 80
  Rebecca, 4
  Shadrack, 52, 53
Cheney
  Joseph, 90
  Richard, 120, 148
  Samuel, 149
Chesley
  John, 142
Chew
  Joseph, 51
Chittam
  Thomas, 97, 109, 111,
    112, 113, 117
Church
  Luke, 70
  Mary, 70
Clagett
  Edward, 25, 51, 123
  John, 27, 123
  Richard, 123
  Thomas, 13, 126
Clark
  Abraham, 67, 82
  Abraham, Jr., 67
  Alice, 124
  John, 40
  Joseph, 122
  Margaret Lee, 124
  Richard, 8
  Thomas, 103, 104, 124,
    145, 164
  Thomas, Jr., 124
Clarke
  George, 25, 57, 147
Clarkson
  Edward, 19, 130

Clifford
  John, 168
  Rachel, 168
Coffer
  Francis, 19, 130
Collard
  Helena, 37
Collings
  James, 8, 127
Conn
  George, Jr., 169
Conner
  Thomas, 57
Contee
  Jane, 128, 131
  John, 65, 164
  John (JP), 8, 10, 18, 27, 33,
    39, 44, 46, 67, 71, 154,
    167
  Theodore, 65, 140
  Thomas, 27, 71
  Thomas (JP), 15, 21, 22,
    52, 66, 67, 68, 81, 92,
    125, 126, 127
Cook
  Robert Dove, 103
Cooke
  John, 138, 139
  John (JP), 23, 26, 30, 48,
    49, 50, 60, 65, 67, 69,
    72, 76, 84, 94, 104, 121,
    140, 141, 151, 152, 165,
    167
Crabb
  Edward, 46, 82, 83
  Jeremiah, 46, 81, 87, 88,
    97
  Lucy, 97

  Priscilla, 82, 83
  Ralph, 82
Crafford
  James, 77, 78
Crafts
  James, 105
Cramphin
  Thomas, 47, 48, 51, 81,
    168
Craufurd
  David, 13, 126, 148
  Mary, 148
Crawford
  George, 23
Cross
  George, 63, 150
  John, 54
  William, 26
Crow
  James, 61, 89, 90, 146
Croxall
  Robert, 120
Daily
  Daniel, 149, 150
Darnall
  Henry, 17, 34, 35, 36, 37,
    38, 47, 86
  Henry, Jr., 128, 131, 153
  Isaac, 56
  John, 86, 107, 153, 160
  John (JP), 107
  Rachel, 128, 131
Davies
  Allen, 127, 128
  Cornelius, 95
Davis
  Ann, 153
  Deborah, 94

175

Ephraim, 153
Nicholas, Jr., 137
Samuel, 45, 94
Thomas, 15, 166
William, 90, 136
Dawson
George, 99
John, 56, 99
Nicholas, 16
Day
Samuel, 145
Deakins
John, 115, 116
Tabitha, 125
William, 20, 21, 45, 46, 71,
72, 98, 99, 108, 118,
119, 125, 134
Demall
John, 133
Dent
Peter, 1, 133
Peter (JP), 7, 18, 20, 22,
26, 33, 39, 40, 42, 43,
44, 45, 61, 71, 89, 117,
135
William, 44, 117
Dick
James, 87
Dickeson
Henry, 40
Thomas, 19
Digges
Edward, 50
Ignatius, 35, 37, 38, 86, 95,
139, 140, 158
Mary, 50
William, 104, 167
William (Potomack), 154

Dixon
George, 42, 43
Dorch
William, 154
Dorsett
John, 134, 162
Mary, 21
Thomas, 21
William, 134
William Newman, 21, 45,
134
Dove
William, 14, 119
William, Jr., 119
Drane
James, 81, 133
Thomas, 165
Drew
Timothy, 6, 17, 47, 162
Dryden
Elizabeth, 84
Ducker
William, 87, 130
Duckett
John, 98
William, 106
Duly
Henry, 14
Duvall
Benjamin (Marsh), 127
Lewis, 61, 141, 142, 145
Mareen, 156
Mary, 127
Maureen, 121
Dyar
Henrietta, 162
Thomas, 161, 162

Foard
    Elizabeth, 14
    William, 14
Ford
    James, 112, 113
Fowler
    Jeremiah, 105, 146
Fraser
    George, 18
    George (JP), 1, 3, 39
Frasier
    Daniel (of Broad Creek),
        169
Frazer
    John, 1, 15
Frolick
    Edmund's, 4
Fry
    James, 135
    Joseph, 33, 135
    Robert, 33
Galloway
    Samuel, 46
Gamblin
    James, 59
Gambra
    James, 59
Gantt
    George, 27
    George (JP), 2, 3, 6, 28, 58,
        59, 65, 67, 68, 76, 77,
        81, 91, 92, 122, 123,
        124, 126, 129, 132, 149,
        151, 153, 164, 165, 166
    Thomas, 165
Gay
    Ruxton, 128

George
    John, 8, 9
    Martha, 8
Ghiselin
    Reverdy, 8
Gibbs
    James, 151, 153
    James, Sr., 151
    William, 151
Gibson
    James, 105
    John, 86, 161
Gittings
    Benjamin, 57
    Phillip, 40
Gordon
    George, 67
    George (JP), 15, 17, 29, 47,
        53, 56, 59, 66, 70, 72,
        76, 77, 92, 93, 98, 104,
        106, 122, 150, 151, 153,
        154, 155, 157, 158, 162,
        163, 164, 171
    Robert, 42
    Thomas, 69, 140
Gore
    James, 142
Goslin
    Ezekiel, 25
Graham
    John, 148
Gray
    Richard, 142
    William, 90, 145, 146
Green
    James, 41, 42, 124
    James, Jr., 124

Greenfield
  Gerard T., 70
  Gerard Truman, 78, 142,
    166
  James Truman, 142
  Nathaniel Truman, 142
  Thomas, 166
  Thomas Smith, 3, 22, 64,
    66
Grimes
  John, 64
Grindall
  John, 68
Groome
  Richard, 46
  William, 21, 46
Hagan
  Margaret, 79, 93
  Thomas, 79, 92, 93, 107
Haggarty
  John, 84, 94
Hall
  Benjamin, 127
  Benjamin s/o Francis, 102
  Francis, 54
  William, 62, 72
Hallam
  John, 165
Halsall
  John, 51, 83
  Pretious, 51
Hamilton
  Andrew, 155, 156
  Thomas, 6, 167
  William, 129
Hammett
  Robert, 74, 75, 91, 98

Hanson
  John, 136
  Samuel, 152
  Walter, 104
Hardey
  George, 59
  George, Jr., 59, 70
  Henry, Jr., 59
  Lucy, 59
  Sarah, 59
Harris
  John, 41
  John, Jr., 41
  John, Sr., 43
Harrison
  J., 61
Harvey
  Eleanor, 167
  James, 52, 167
  Thomas, 162
Harvie
  William, 12
Harwood
  Sarah, 149
  Thomas, 50, 68, 89, 106,
    149
Hawkins
  Henry Smith, 135, 136
  John, 7
  John Stone, 4, 60, 61, 63
  John, Jr., 95
  Mary, 73
  William, 12
Healy
  John, 143, 144, 165, 168
  Mary Ann, 143
Hebb
  William (JP), 55, 56

John, 32, 33
Hunter
  William, 19
Hutchison
  William, 44
Hutton
  Margaret, 85
  Richard, 7, 18, 27, 28, 84,
    85, 94, 127, 137
Hyde
  John, 34, 35, 36, 38
  Samuel, 34
Isaac
  Richard, 61, 89, 90, 130,
    145, 146
  Richard, Jr., 61, 89, 90,
    130, 146
  Richard, Sr., 145, 146
  Sarah, 130
Jackson
  Alexander, 18, 26
Jacob
  Benjamin, 130
  Jemima, 102, 131, 168
  Mordecai, 44, 130
  Mordecai (JP), 6, 16, 17,
    26, 30, 32, 45, 46, 52,
    54, 61, 62, 63, 64, 68,
    69, 76, 81, 83, 87, 88,
    94, 95, 96, 97, 102, 104,
    105, 109, 120, 121, 125,
    127, 129, 130, 131, 141,
    144, 147, 148, 149, 151,
    158, 160, 161, 168, 169
Jenkins
  Daniel, 154
  Enoch, 153, 154
  John, 103

Ruth, 154
Sarah, 77
William, 27, 60
William of Piscattaway
  Hundred, 60
Johnson
  Bernard, 85, 94
  John, 14
Johnstown
  John, 23
Jones
  George, 64
  John, 39, 40
  Joseph, 144, 147
  Notley, 38, 39
  Richard, 45, 93, 94
Keene
  Richard, 37
Kelly
  Elizabeth, 67
Kent
  Robert, 33
Kersby
  John, 120
King
  Francis, 22, 33, 40
  Henry, 148
  Thomas, 46, 66
Kirkwood
  Richard, 80
Lamar
  John, Jr., 160, 161
  Sarah, 160, 161
Lancaster
  Thomas, 129
Lang
  John, 76

Thomas, 55, 74, 75, 91, 98, 125, 162
Northey
  Samuel, 107
Norton
  Alexander, 19, 136, 137
  John, 78
Notley
  Thomas, 86
O'Brian
  Terrence, 41, 43
Offutt
  Nathaniel, 23, 30, 31, 32, 138
Oliver
  Elizabeth, 67
  Leonard, 29, 32, 33, 67
Orme
  Aaron, 46
  James, 28
  John, 28, 142, 158, 167
  John (Rev), 158
  John (Reverend), 28
  John, Sr., 134
  Moses, 34, 35, 36, 65, 70
  Moses, Jr., 142, 143
  Ruth, 28
  Verlinda, 142, 143
Osborn
  Edward, 83
Ouchterlony
  John, 167
Padgett
  Thomas, 9
Page
  Daniel, 45, 108
Panner
  John, 164

Parker
  Ann, 77, 92
  Gabriel, 77, 92
  George, 56, 79, 92, 143, 153
  Sarah, 77
Parmer
  John, 121, 122
  Mary, 121, 122
Parnham
  John, 40
Peach
  Joseph, 96
  Joseph, Jr., 96, 112
  Joseph, Sr., 112
Pearce
  William, 10
Pelley
  James, 118, 152
Pelly
  James, 52, 152
Penson
  William, 19, 39
Perrie
  John, 127, 128
  Samuel, 85, 128
Perry
  Edward, 169
  Joseph, 129
Peter
  Robert, 77, 159, 160
Phelps
  Walter, 106
Pickerell
  Elizabeth, 58, 59
  Ralph, 58, 59
Pierce
  John, 10

148, 155, 157, 159

Willocy
    Philip, 8
Willson
    Elizabeth, 29
    James, 18, 117
    John, 84, 94
    Jonathan, 94
    Josias, 29
    Lancelot, 84
    Martha, 94
Wilmot
    John, Jr., 144, 147
Wilsford
    Henry, 13
Wilson
    Hugh, 152
    James, 32
    John, 9
    Joseph, 30
    Lancelot, 30, 120, 167
    Mary, 30, 32
    Thomas, 84
Windham
    William, 65
Windsor
    Luke, 56
Wood
    James, 149
    John, 129
    Sacheverell, 73

Thomas, Sr., 133
Woodward
    Abraham, 133
Woolsford
    Henry, 13
Wootton
    Elizabeth, 29, 30
    Turner, 29, 30, 50, 101,
        102, 105, 106, 157, 158,
        161
    William Turner, 5, 129
    William Turnor, 29
Wright
    Henry, 146
    Jane, 80
    Joseph, 17
    Richard, 80
    Samuel, 17
Yates
    Charles, 93
    Joseph, 33, 140
Yoe
    Stephen, 27, 28
Young
    Anne, 86, 88, 89
    James, 14
    Mary, 56, 63
    Molly, 56
    William, 2, 10, 12, 105,
        114, 116

www.ingramcontent.com/pod-product-compliance
Lightning Source LLC
Chambersburg PA
CBHW070914270326
41927CB00011B/2564